'Remi Adekoya is a welcome bla[...] race debate clogged up with emo[...] of the economic underpinnings [...] hierarchies will make uncomfort[...] conservatives'   David Goodhart

'This terrifically illuminating book . . . offers a new way of understanding modern racial structures'   *i Newspaper*

'This is a courageous and urgent intervention into one of the most important debates of our time- one in which we often seem curiously incurious about what would lead to genuine equality among groups. In clear and elegant prose Dr. Adekoya will shift the way you think about hierarchies of race'
                                    Thomas Chatterton Williams

'Remi brings a unique international perspective to the race debate, allowing the reader to understand complexities in the discussion that they won't have considered before'
                                    Katharine Birbalsingh

'Adekoya's book is one of the rare works which problematize the Woke stereotypes: it correctly grounds "racist prejudices" in wealth differences. All sincere liberal anti-racists should read this book to grasp why their efforts are so counterproductive. And since liberal anti-racism is the hegemonic ideology in our countries, this means that EVERYBODY should read Adekoya's book'   Slavoj Žižek

'*It's Not About Whiteness, It's About Wealth* form[s] part of the urgent and long-awaited intellectual work needed to create a genuinely fair and socially just society, one that doesn't depend on treating ethnic minority people like children . . . The strength of Adekoya's book is that it is rooted in concrete, material questions in the context of a debate transfixed by the performative and the representational'   *Critic*

'Adekoya provides a vital international dimension to these questions [around race]'   *Literary Review Magazine*

Remi Adekoya is a politics lecturer at the University of York. He is a former journalist and has written for *Guardian, Sunday Times, New Statesman, Washington Post, Foreign Policy, Foreign Affairs, Politico, Spectator, Evening Standard,* and *UnHerd* among others. He has provided sociopolitical analysis and commentary for CNN, BBC, Sky News, Al Jazeera, Canadian Broadcasting Corporation (CBC), South African Broadcasting Corporation (SABC), African International Television (AIT), Radio France International (RFI), Talk Radio and Times Radio, among others. He is the author of *Biracial Britain*.

It's Not About Whiteness, It's About Wealth

How the economics of race really work

Remi Adekoya

CONSTABLE

CONSTABLE

First published in Great Britain in 2023 by Constable
This paperback edition published in 2024 by Constable

1 3 5 7 9 10 8 6 4 2

A CIP catalogue record for this book
is available from the British Library.

ISBN: 978-1-40871-667-0 (hardback)

Typeset in Minion by SX Composing DTP, Rayleigh, Essex
Printed and bound in Great Britain by Clays Ltd, Elcograf, S.p.A.

Papers used by Constable are from well-managed forests
and other responsible sources.

Constable
An imprint of
Little, Brown Book Group
Carmelite House
50 Victoria Embankment
London EC4Y 0DZ

An Hachette UK Company

www.hachette.co.uk

www.littlebrown.co.uk

I dedicate this book to my wife and daughter.
You are what gives my life meaning.

Contents

Introduction:

What children see

In 2011, a group of psychologists decided to investigate the racial attitudes of children in South Africa. A diverse group of primary-school kids aged four to nine were presented photographs of people representing various racial groups and asked to point to who they 'liked'. It turned out black, white and 'coloured' (multiracial) children all favoured white people.[1]

While earlier studies in other multiracial societies had revealed similar pro-white biases among children, these had all been conducted in Europe and North America. It had been assumed children in those places favoured whites because they were the dominant *majority group* upheld as the norm. This was obviously not the case in South Africa, which was 80 per cent black and just 9 per cent white. While such pro-white biases may have been unsurprising during the apartheid era where the state openly glorified whiteness, these kids were growing up under black presidents and governments in a South Africa that emphasised racial equality. A country whose most respected individual was a black man by the name of Nelson Mandela.

The authors of the study suggested the children's pro-white biases could be motivated by their perceptions of *group status* in South Africa. Research has shown children favour higher-status groups over lower-status ones. Hispanic kids favour whites over African Americans. African American kids favour whites over Hispanics. White Australian kids favour Asians over Aborigines. Taiwanese kids favour whites over blacks. And British-Asian kids have been shown to favour whites over British-Caribbean kids while the latter favoured whites over British-Asians.[2]

The question then was *what criteria* South African kids were using to assess group status in their society? It clearly wasn't group size. Their preferences appeared to mirror the country's wealth hierarchy, but was it possible children that age even noticed who owned what? Subsequent studies revealed they did. Presented pictures of nice houses and fancy cars juxtaposed with images of shacks and beat-up jalopies, children as young as three matched the expensive possessions first to whites and then to multiracials while often associating the shacks and jalopies with black people.[3] At the time, average income for white South African households was three times that of multiracial households and seven times that of black households, so the kids were accurately noting the correlation between race and wealth in their country.

This mattered in shaping their attitudes towards various groups as further research revealed that they *preferred* the affluent. Presented pictures of expensively dressed children in fancy houses and poorly dressed children in shabby ones, irrespective whether they themselves were black or white, or from rich or poor homes, the children 'liked' the affluent kids more and were keener to befriend them.[4] Shown two black kids, one presented as rich, the other as poor, they preferred the rich black kid. Similar studies in America have shown primary-school children can distinguish between 'rich' and 'poor' people in photographs, generally favour the rich and associate wealth with whiteness and poverty with blackness.

Five-year-olds are obviously too young to have developed any coherently classist worldviews, so psychologists have pondered why they gravitate towards the better-off. Some suggest they are simply attracted by the aesthetically pleasing possessions money can buy and transfer the wow feelings they experience at the sight of a shiny toy or sleek car onto their owners. Others think they perceive potential benefits from being around affluent kids, such as being allowed to play with their fancy toys.

One study in two very economically and culturally different environments – the US and India – showed American children from predominantly middle-class families and Indian children from lower-income families both believed children from wealthy homes were 'likelier to share' than children from poor homes.[5] Likely because they were assuming kids from wealthy homes simply have more available to share and can do so at less cost than those who have little. It is easier for a kid with five toy cars to offer his peers one of them to play with than it is for a kid with only one toy car to give it up for someone else.

Whatever the underlying factors behind these dynamics, such findings 'reveal children's sensitivity to information that is *ubiquitous in society*, but often neglected by those interested in the development of social attitudes and stereotypes', one study concluded.[6] In today's race debate, it would seem we are either neglecting the obvious or unwilling to discuss it frankly and in detail.

Much of the anger and frustration around race today is driven by popular feelings that racial hierarchies still permeate our world. That while no longer formalised as during apartheid, colonialism, or slavery, we continue to live in a world in which white people are generally positioned at the top, black people at the bottom and everyone else somewhere in between, an order that has been with us for some five hundred years now. This feeling is particularly strong within the group that feels stuck at the bottom.

A 2020 CNN survey of UK ethnic minorities revealed that on issues ranging from police treatment to chances of life success in Britain, 'the results are striking; it is often the case that black people are considerably more dissatisfied with race relations than other ethnic minorities'.[7] For instance, 69 per cent of black people in Britain believed they have fewer opportunities to succeed professionally than white people, compared with 49 per cent of non-black minorities. An ITV poll that same year showed black people were the most likely to describe Britain's police, justice system, education system, parliament and corporate world, as well as sports, arts and beauty industries, as plagued by a 'culture of racism'.[8] A 2021 Ipsos survey confirmed the trend of black people seeing themselves as the most unfairly treated group in Britain.[9]

Meanwhile, in the US, a 2021 Pew Research study showed 58 per cent of African Americans believe that to achieve racial equality in their country 'most US laws and institutions need to be completely rebuilt as they are fundamentally biased'.[10]

4

In comparison, 30 per cent of Hispanics and 24 per cent of Asian Americans believe such a radical overhaul necessary, meaning black Americans are at least twice as likely to believe the system is currently rigged against them as these other major non-white groups. In a 2019 survey, more than half – 52 per cent – of black adults in America said being black has 'hurt their ability to get ahead', compared to a quarter of Hispanics and Asians (24 per cent each).[11]

Black dissatisfaction with the status quo is not restricted to those living in Britain and America or even the West. In recent years, the Black Lives Matter slogan has also resonated with Africans living in Africa who have never met a white police officer and face no personal racism in their daily lives. Their day-to-day struggles are very different from those of the black person in Britain or America. Yet following major events that bring the race issue to the fore, such as the killing of George Floyd in 2020, they unite with the black diaspora in a shared sense of global disregard for blackness. Their sentiments, while consciously intensified and exploited by race activists, *are* reflective of the global reality.

Whether it is Libyans selling black Africans into slavery in the twenty-first century, Chinese people paying $70 to watch videos of Malawian children made to chant 'I'm a monster. My IQ is low',[12] or Indians openly discriminating against black people in their country,[13] a general disregard for blackness appears to be a constant. A 2021 UN report found discrimination against black people happens pretty much everywhere outside Africa.[14]

Hence, while various groups complain of a persisting racial hierarchy, it is the particularly stark contrast between the position of black and white that is really driving today's increasingly bitter and polarised race debate. It is no coincidence that today's antiracism movement is driven by intellectuals and activists of black descent.

The story of how the current racial order emerged is one we are familiar with – the Trans-Atlantic slave trade, colonialism, Western imperialism, and the ideology of white supremacy were all key to establishing its ranking. The issue today is what is sustaining this now informal order despite the plethora of moral and intellectual arguments levelled against it over the years? Why has it not ended when so many say they are completely against it? If a human phenomenon most people say is wrong persists, it means there must be something very powerful keeping it going. Something capable of truncating all our best intentions.

All hierarchies reflect differences in power and status, so I believe the key question here is what gives some racial groups more power and status than others? When I refer to 'power', I mean the ability to influence events, environments and people. By *influence*, I mean being able to have an effect on what happens, what places are like and how people think and behave. Whether that effect is 'positive' or 'negative' is up to the beholder; as long as an effect has occurred, influence has been exercised and power has been exerted.

Understood this way, it's clear everyone has *some* power in this world as we are all able to influence some events, environments and people in our lives. Where individuals and groups have come to differ vastly, and what is causing much frustration, is in the *degree* and *scope* of their power in this world. This will be the subject of this book with regards to the race equation. When I refer to 'status' in the book, I simply mean where others position us as individuals or groups in the grand scheme of things. The fact that our status depends not on how we see ourselves but on how others see us is a crucial dynamic in the whole equation. A writer's literary status, for instance, has nothing to do with what the writer thinks of their writing and everything to do with what others think of it.

In this book, I argue that the chief source of racial group power and status today is collective wealth. It is not the only thing that matters, but it is the thing that matters the most in a capitalist world. Money creates and sustains hierarchies. I say this not out of anti-capitalist feeling, merely as a statement of fact. In a system that runs on money, the distribution of wealth shapes the distribution of power. I will thus be looking at how wealth influences racial dynamics in several key domains of our modern world, ranging from immigration, knowledge, technology and media to group stereotypes, allocation of prestige and international power.

This is not just about the raw purchasing power money provides, it is also very much about the meaning people assign to wealth and the qualities they attribute to those who wield it. The material dynamics of race relations shape their psychological dynamics, but the latter are no less important in the current equation. If five-year-olds are already forming attitudes towards groups shaped by whether they see them as haves or have-nots, how much more so adults navigating a world in which pretty much everything costs money?

A lot has been said about 'whiteness' in recent years in the name of dismantling white supremacy. In my view, too much of it is based on wishful thinking, as I shall strive to evidence in this book.

The race equation resembles what it resembles today not because the ideology of white supremacy is so diabolically clever it continues to bamboozle the world for no logical reason. We are where we are because the current global order has a very solid structural foundation. Racism does not explain its persistence, the solidity of that foundation does.

We live in a world in which single European states like Britain and Germany have larger economies than Africa, a continent of 1.4 billion people and home to roughly 90 per cent of the world's black population. If you created a single economy comprising *all* the sixty-plus black-majority countries in the world, including the Caribbean nations, their combined GDP still wouldn't amount to Germany's $4 trillion figure.

We can debate colonialism, slavery, and Western imperialism *in perpetuum*, but that won't change the economic realities of our world. Nor will arguing that the West would never have got to where it is today if not for its exploitative past make whites any poorer, less powerful, or less high-status in the eyes of the world. Despite all the talk of white exploitation and racism over the years, whiteness continues to enjoy a defiant glow such accusations appear incapable of diminishing. A race debate not embedded in detailed material realities is intellectual masturbation.

It is high time for a relentless focus on the realities sustaining global hierarchies and how they manifest in our everyday lives. To be effective, this requires a more global view of racial dynamics than the parochial Anglo-American lens that dominates today's race debate on both left and right. What happens in Britain and America matters as these are both influential countries, but events in London and New York are not going to decide the future of global race relations.

Less than 3 per cent of the world's black population currently live in the US and UK combined. Moreover, this proportion will most likely shrink as Africa's population is set to double to 2.5 billion by 2050.[15] For some perspective, there are already five times more Nigerians than black Americans and Nigeria's population will surpass that of the entire United States by 2050. The West is also home to but a tiny proportion of other non-white populations likewise unhappy with the current order. The demographic reality is such that it is global-scale dynamics which will shape the future of race relations, not their manifestations in this or that Western society, however important.

I will use the term 'racial groups' in this book quite often even though it is a highly imprecise term. There are 1.4 billion Indians, but it is not clear if they are to be considered a distinct racial group or categorised as 'brown' people, as folk from South Asia and the Middle East are often talked about. When I do use the term 'racial groups', it should be understood to refer to groups of people who are popularly identified and treated *as if* they were members of a same 'race'.

When I refer to 'brown', 'black', or 'white' people, it is simply in the spirit of reflecting how the complicatedly diverse peoples of this world are racially categorised in popular perceptions. This book is generally very focused on the role of mass sentiments in race relations as these affect people's everyday lives more than the views of particular individuals here and there, myself included, of course.

As for me, I was born and raised in Nigeria to a Nigerian father and Polish mother, rendering me a first-hand witness to the black–white dynamic from my earliest years. My wife is Nigerian, and my daughter British Nigerian, so I have a vested interest in the present and future status of blackness. I write this from that perspective. I identify strongly with the African continent in its entirety, though I also lived in my mother's homeland for many years and have called Britain home since 2015. My formative experiences growing up in Lagos were key to shaping my understanding of how the world works, black perceptions of whiteness and the power of money. Living in the rich North and in the often much poorer South are two vastly different experiences bound to shape your worldview quite differently. I have lived both here and there and draw my observations from both worlds.

While other groups will be discussed where context demands it, my main focus will be on the dynamics between black and white as I firmly believe it is the interplay between these two that will continue to drive the race debate in this century. I hope to shed some light on how collective wealth shapes racial status in everyday life and what the future holds for the current order.

1

A picture of racial wealth

Our world is organised into national economies that are constantly being measured against each other. News reports will regularly inform us of how Britain is now (not) the fastest-growing economy in Europe, Nigeria is Africa's largest economy or China's GDP looks set to surpass America's in such and such year. We hear of which economies are doing well and which are doing badly.

While nations are made up of diverse groups, virtually all the nations in the world contain a clear racial majority. Britain is 82 per cent white. Nine in ten of Europe's inhabitants are white.[1] Even in the US, by far the most racially diverse Western nation, whites constitute 71 per cent of the population.[2] While the West has no doubt undergone significant demographic changes in recent decades, it remains a predominantly white world. Conversely, Africa is predominantly black, containing, as mentioned earlier, nine in ten of the world's black people.

In terms of the other major racial-cum-identity categories often spoken about, 'Asians' are obviously from a huge collection of nations, and range from the Chinese to the Indians and more than a few in between. Nevertheless, the average global citizen will likely distinguish chiefly between those who hail from the Middle East (often referred to as the 'Arab world' even though many other groups inhabit the region), South Asians and East Asians. And of course, there is the popular belief in the existence of a 'Latino' group, chiefly located in South America. It is thus possible, based on available national and international data, to draw a picture of 'racial' wealth that is broadly reflective of our global reality.

While the economic rise of some non-white nations, chiefly in Asia, is undoubtedly reshaping the world order, the upper echelons of the global economy remain dominated by white-majority nations. Despite being home to just 17 per cent of the world's population, Europe and North America still account for roughly half of its $101 trillion GDP. Six of the ten largest economies in the world today are white-majority nations.

As at 2022, Sweden, a country of ten million people, generated a GDP of $603 billion compared to $504 billion for Nigeria, the largest black nation, with 214 million inhabitants.[3] Tiny Ireland, with its five million citizens, had a GDP of $520 billion in comparison to $411 billion in the case of South Africa, the most industrialised black-majority nation with a population of sixty million. The economic gap is not just between black and white, of course.

Norway's five-million-strong economy boasts a GDP of $505 billion against the $461 billion generated by Bangladesh, which has 170 million people. Nine million Swiss citizens live in an $807-billion economy, more than twice the size of Pakistan's $376 billion GDP, despite the latter having a population of 235 million. Britain's economy is roughly equal to India's in size despite the latter having twenty times more citizens and generally being on the rise in recent years.

The differences are most visible in GDP per capita figures, crucial to gauging the average living standards and buying power of individual citizens: sixteen of the twenty nations with the highest GDP per capita in the world are white-majority countries.[4] At the other end, eighteen of the twenty countries with the lowest GDP per capita are black-majority nations. Luxembourg has a GDP per capita 471 times that of Burundi – $125,923 compared to $267.

For a broader picture, thirty-three of the fifty nations with the highest per capita GDP are white majority while thirty of the fifty with the lowest are black majority. There is not a single white-majority nation in the poorest-fifty group; all are non-white. Of course, there are major economic differences *between* white-majority nations, with UK GDP per capita standing at $42k compared to $15k in Romania. However, an indication of just how better-off than most others white-majority countries are, is the fact that China, despite its ongoing economic miracle, still ranks lower than Romania, Croatia or Hungary in terms of per capita GDP, even though these countries are relatively poor by European standards.

The fact that Britain has a GDP per capita of $42k (£33k) does not by any means translate to everyone in the UK earning £33k a year. These are average economic output figures which obscure often significant disparities *within* rich societies and there are plenty of complaints about that. But they do give us a snapshot of the economic strength of these nations compared to others. Sub-Saharan Africa is the poorest region in the world with a GDP per capita of $1.8k, compared to Europe's $34k and North America's $57k.[5] In between those extremes, the figure stands at $2.4k for South Asia, $8.7k for South America, $17k for East Asia and $19k for the Middle East region.

The World Bank defines the global 'middle class' as those earning at least $12,535 a year, which comes out to just over $1k a month. This may seem a modest income to Westerners – which just shows how much richer than others they are – but sounds about right in a global context. As of today, eight in ten Europeans and nine in ten North Americans reach this global middle-class income threshold.[6] In China it is one in four. In Latin America it's one in six and in the Middle East it's one in nine. In South Asia and Africa, where most of the world's black and brown populations are concentrated, just one in fifty people – *2 per cent* of the population – have monthly incomes exceeding $1k. Britain has a larger number of people qualifying as global middle class than the whole of Africa or South Asia.

Future trends bode well for China, which is expected to see its share of citizens with global middle-class incomes double to 52 per cent by 2030, while South Asia's share is also expected to double (but to a much more modest 4 per cent). The proportion in South America is expected to inch up to 18 per cent while the figure in Africa is expected to remain stagnant – at a mere 2 per cent. This is because while African economies are expected to grow, their populations are growing even faster, which means that while there will be more collective income, there will also be many more around to share it.

The differences are even more glaring when it comes to levels of household wealth in the world's regions. By the end of 2021, global household wealth totalled an estimated $464 trillion.[7] North America and Europe together account for 57 per cent of total household wealth, again, despite containing just 17 per cent of the world's adult population. North American households held $158 trillion while European households held $106 trillion. Chinese households held $85 trillion, households in the Asia Pacific region held $81 trillion, Indian households $14 trillion, while South American households boasted $12 trillion in wealth. African households were by far the collective poorest, holding $6 trillion in wealth.

If all the household wealth in North America was converted into its cash value and distributed equally among its inhabitants, each adult in the region would receive a cheque for $561k. Respectively, each European would pocket $180k, while their Chinese and Asian-Pacific counterparts could count on $77k and $65k. Each South American adult would receive $28k and each Indian adult $15k. Each African would receive $8k. For the record, if all the world's wealth was distributed equally among its adults irrespective of country of origin, each individual would get $87k.

Of the twenty countries with the highest median wealth per adult in the world, fourteen were white-majority nations. Britain was number nine, just ahead of France and behind Netherlands. Median wealth per adult in the UK was eighty-three times what it was in Nigeria, forty-one times what it was in India, thirty-eight times what it was in Brazil, twenty-seven times what it was in South Africa and five times what it was in China. Millionaires are extremely rare in the global South, around one in a thousand adults in India and Indonesia and one in two hundred in China. In the likes of Italy and Spain, your chances of encountering a millionaire at random rise to one in thirty-three, in Britain, it's one in twenty, in the US, one in eleven and in Switzerland, one in six.

Household wealth *grew* in the West during the Coronavirus pandemic. Aside from the fact people spent less than usual because they stayed indoors, rich-country citizens received massive government support via furloughs, cheques in the mail and whatnot. Poor-country citizens could count on no such largesse when their economies froze to a standstill. To live in a poor country is to be dealt a double whammy – you will likely have very little money and so will your government. Britain wields a national budget of a trillion pounds, thirty-three times the size of Nigeria's budget, despite the latter having well over three times more people.[8] The UK's budget is more than double that of India, which again, has twenty times more people.[9]

Ethiopia, Africa's second-largest nation with a population of 115 million, wielded a national budget of $13 billion in 2021. For education, healthcare, infrastructure, everything. Slovakia, which has five million people and is hardly a rich country by European standards, had a budget twice that size.[10] The picture in terms of per capita budget figures mirrors that of GDP per capita figures with white-majority nations generally dominating the upper ranks along with a few wealthy East Asian states, while most governments of the global South have very scarce resources per citizen to spend on providing healthcare, education, infrastructure, and other social needs.

As a result, during the pandemic, people in the global South had to draw on whatever savings they had to survive, causing household wealth to shrink in many black and brown nations, further exacerbating the racial wealth gap. The Covid experience was a great example of the role collective white wealth plays in advantaging white people over most of the rest of the world.

What worsens the racial wealth gap of course is that even within rich Western societies the big-picture hierarchy tends to be replicated, with white people having the most, black people the least, and everyone else somewhere in between. The median white British household is worth £314,000 compared to £34,000 for the median black African household.[11] In between these two extremes are the other racial groups, with British Indians being the exceptional case of a group whose typical wealth matches that of whites.

The pattern repeats itself in America where the typical white family owns five times the wealth of the typical Hispanic family and eight times that of the typical black family.[12] The black and white wealth gap in America is as wide today as it was in the 1960s.[13] These are the Western nations that compile detailed racial wealth statistics; others don't. I would, however, risk a guess that the racial wealth hierarchy in all Western nations is not ordered much differently than in the UK and the US, especially with regards to who sits atop and at bottom.

Neither is the racial wealth gap restricted to Western countries. In South America, where 133 million 'Afro-descendants' constitute the largest black population outside Africa, they are overrepresented among the poor in every country.[14] In Brazil, where the largest group lives, they are twice as likely to be poor as white Brazilians. Even in Uruguay, one of the most egalitarian nations in Latin America, Afro-Uruguayans are three times more likely to be poor.

Afro-descendants are about twice as likely to live in slums as non-Afro-descendants in Brazil, Colombia, Costa Rica, Ecuador, Mexico and Uruguay. Regionally, they are over two and a half times more likely to live in chronic poverty than whites or Mestizos. During the first half of the twentieth century in Colombia, 'black' was even used as a way of referring to poor groups, even if they were not black, so synonymous was blackness with poverty! The South Americans descended from European ancestors are at the top of the economic hierarchy while blacks are at the bottom.

I am discussing here racial wealth gaps which are of course different from *racial income* gaps that also exist but are narrowing in many cases. In Britain, there is now a higher percentage of British Indians and British Chinese in the top income quintile (top fifth of earners) after housing costs than British whites, with the figures standing at 24 per cent, 22 per cent, and 21 per cent respectively.[15] The figure is 8 per cent for black Britons and 4 per cent for British Pakistanis. Similar trends are observable in the US where, for instance, Asian women and men have been shown to earn more than their white, black and Hispanic counterparts.[16]

One striking US study in 2018 showed that black Americans' disadvantage on social mobility relative to whites is entirely driven by a disadvantage between black and white *men*.[17] No matter what their parents' income level, black men do worse than white men on average in today's America, but the same does not hold for black women. While the study still found white women earning more on average than black women, in this case, the gap could be explained by differences in family background. 'Conditional on their parents' income, black women actually outperform white women in terms of individual earnings,' the study noted.

There are a myriad national and even regional-specific factors affecting income inequalities between groups today. It would be simplistic nonsense to boil them all down to one factor, such as racism, for instance, as some would have. However, discussing the *reasons* for income inequalities today would require a whole book all on its own. I am focused here on current wealth levels and how they sustain group hierarchies in the big picture as it stands.

While inflation and the cost-of-living crisis have undoubtedly affected people's finances negatively since 2022, including obviously in the wealth sphere, this has been a global phenomenon, not one restricted to the West. The global picture today thus remains one in which whites enjoy the collective status of an economic aristocracy, while blacks, along with other significantly poorer non-white groups, are often viewed as members of a global economic underclass, even if a few have made good. Race is the primordial manifestation of this global order. It has come to indicate group status within it while skin colour is the cue people use to make snap judgements about who is likely positioned where, who is giving the orders, who is taking them, who works for whom, who is important and who isn't. The human propensity for making snap judgements combined with the high visibility of skin colour leads to situations such as that of Edward Enninful, the first black British editor of the prestigious *Vogue* magazine, who was told by a security guard who didn't know who he was to 'use the loading bay' as he entered its London office in 2021.

The incident typified the kind of encounters that often infuriate black- or brown-skinned professionals who are mistaken for 'the help' in upper-sphere environments in the West. While these are clearly cases of racial stereotyping as Enninful described it, their psychological roots are to be found in the *general associations* of blackness with low status everywhere outside Africa. Drawing attention to such incidents on social media is likely to increase the probability of people being more careful about publicly making such assumptions in the future, but it will not necessarily stop the world associating blackness with low status per se.

And because of the high visibility of skin colour and the fact race is often *emphasised as a differentiating factor here in the West*, black status in Britain (or America) cannot be divorced from black status in the wider world. While its everyday manifestations are always shaped by local contexts, cultures and histories, the racial order is an *international order*, as Immanuel Wallerstein, the late Yale University sociologist, aptly observed.

A white man who walks into a Nigerian office building will be presumed a businessman or some sort of visiting professional by a Nigerian security guard. He is unlikely to be mistaken for a delivery courier for the simple reason it is highly unlikely there are *any* white delivery couriers working in Nigeria. No white person need leave their country to go work for the $150-a-month salary the job pays in Nigeria. You generally won't find many white people doing menial or other low-paid jobs in non-white countries, but you will find many black and brown people doing them in white-majority countries. That is the economic dynamic we live in, one which builds all sorts of pictures and assumptions in people's heads.

A PICTURE OF RACIAL WEALTH

In the eyes of most of the world, whiteness is presumed wealthy until proven otherwise. This is especially the case *outside* the West. People who live in Britain, America or Canada know that there are more than a few poor white people around. However, as I observed growing up in Lagos, to the Nigerian who has never travelled to the white man's land, there is no such creature as a poor white person. This presumption is intensified by the fact that the white-majority nations people are most familiar with there are the richest ones – the Britains, the Frances, the Germanys, the Canadas, the Australias and of course America.

These are the nations people around the whole world are familiar with either because they were colonised by them or because they dominate global news. When people in Africa think of 'white countries', they're not thinking of Belarus or Bulgaria. It is the association of whiteness primarily with these super-rich Western societies that sustains the perception white equals wealthy, a perception rooted in concrete realities, of course.

Hence, if a magic potion was discovered today that could change your skin colour overnight, it is more difficult to imagine white people choosing to be black or brown than it is to imagine some black and brown people choosing to be white. Not because of a belief being white makes you an inherently better human being but out of the pragmatic assumption whiteness equals status and opportunity. And while it is certainly not the case that all or even nearly all white people enjoy status and opportunity, they are statistically more likely to enjoy both than members of any other racial group. This enhances white prestige and helps perpetuate a particular racial order.

The economic-cum-racial status quo was not divinely ordained and is certainly not inevitable. While it has been remarkably stable for centuries, especially with regards to those positioned at top and bottom, there have been shifts within it and we can expect plenty more this century. The Japanese are probably the most prominent example of a non-white group that is a now long-standing member of the global economic aristocracy.

Back in the 1960s – the heyday of apartheid – the possibility of a $250 million trade deal with then-booming Japan prompted South Africa's racist government to rethink its race calculus. 'Tokyo's Yawata Iron & Steel Co. offered to purchase 5,000,000 tons of South African pig iron . . . With such a huge deal in the works, South Africa could hardly afford to insult the visiting Japanese trade delegations that would now regularly visit the country. Without hesitation, it announced that all Japanese henceforth would be considered white,' a 1962 article in *Time* magazine reported.[18]

This was when the concept of 'honorary whites' first emerged. A country whose laws were based on the claimed permanence of genetic categories found itself rewriting genetics in the face of economic reality, a lesson on the humbling capacity of money. South Korea is another nation that has greatly multiplied its wealth in the past half-century, as have Taiwan and Singapore.

Not coincidentally, the South Koreans and Taiwanese were also offered 'honorary white' status by South Africa's apartheid government, but the Koreans severed diplomatic ties with them in the 1970s anyway in protest at their racist policies, a stance worth remembering for the history books.

Nevertheless, these rich East Asian states have a combined population of 200 million people, which is a fraction of East Asia's 1.7 billion population, and less than 5 per cent of wider Asia's total 4.6 billion population.

This is not, as yet, enough to propel East Asianness, much less Asianness as a whole, to aristocrat status in the eyes of the world. However, once their nationality has been *made known*, citizens of the rich East Asian states are treated differently from others in their region. Same applies to the likes of the Saudis, Qataris, Kuwaitis and Emiratis who come from very wealthy nations today but represent a tiny proportion of the 'Arab world', so Arabness or Middle Easternness is not instinctively associated with wealth today.

I know this could all sound a bit iffy to the Westerner. Could so much of this race stuff really just boil down to money? Do people really base their treatment of others on how much wealth they think they have? Westerners *of all skin colours* do not truly grasp how important wealth is to the race debate because they tend to have different attitudes to money than the rest of the world.

2

Attitudes to money

Despite currently unfavourable economic times, the average Westerner still enjoys a much higher income than most others in the world and is surrounded by people in a usually similar financial situation. Jobs are available. People have access to credit. Those who do not have any income can rely on the state for welfare. Food banks are common as are charity organisations to help those in need. Those who live in Europe have access to well-funded public healthcare systems, of which the NHS is perhaps the most famous example. Access to a good education is widespread and often publicly funded. Even when it is not, a wide variety of scholarships is usually available for those determined to get a good education.

The Westerner lives in a society focused on individual self-fulfilment, not on the fulfilment of obligation to family. While they will obviously need to take care of their children if they do decide to have them, they will usually not have financial demands made on them by extended family members or anyone else. Perhaps a friend might occasionally want to borrow some money or have their drinks paid for on a night out, but people around them will generally be able to cover their basic expenses and won't need financial help from them.

The Westerner also lives in a society that is very attached to the idea of equality, a society that expects people to be treated the same and is often incensed when this is not the case. Europe is the most economically equal continent in the world, with the top 10 per cent receiving 35 per cent of income.[1] All this leads the Westerner to view wealth quite differently from the rest of the world.

A 2021 survey of seven Western nations – the US, UK, Germany, France, Sweden, Italy and Spain – showed an average of 28 per cent of people consider it 'important' for them personally to become rich.[2] The British placed the lowest value on being wealthy with less than a fifth – 19 per cent – saying this was personally important to them. Contrary to pop-culture portrayals of Americans as uber-materialists, only 30 per cent of them prioritise wealth. More Spaniards (31 per cent), Swedes (32 per cent) and Italians (36 per cent) said it was important for them to become rich. Who would have thought more Swedes want to become rich than Americans?

However, the same survey carried out in four key Asian nations – Japan, China, South Korea and Vietnam – showed an average of 58 per cent consider it important for them to become rich, making them twice as likely as Westerners to prioritise money. In each of these Asian nations, more people consider being rich important than in the West. In Japan, 43 per cent feel this way, in China it's 50 per cent, in South Korea it's 63 per cent and in Vietnam it's 76 per cent.

It is symptomatic that even the people from the Asian nations which have been wealthy for decades now – the Japanese and South Koreans – are still more money-focused than Westerners. And based on people's characterisations of the rich, ranging from them being 'superficial', 'ruthless', 'selfish', 'arrogant' and 'greedy' to 'intelligent', 'visionary', 'industrious' and 'optimistic', the study also revealed that most Asians have far more positive attitudes towards the rich than Westerners, with the French and Germans being the most likely to have negative views of wealthy people.

Interestingly, while the Chinese are also far keener on becoming rich than Westerners, their views of wealthy people are less positive than those of other Asians and more in line with those in the West. This is perhaps as a result of the often highly brutal nature of Chinese capitalism and the fact that the wealthiest Chinese are often seen as having become so rich thanks to connections with the Chinese Communist party that controls the economy rather than sheer talent or hard work. Which brings us to the significant question of who people think 'deserves' to be rich.

In the West, rich entrepreneurs and the self-employed are deemed most deserving of their wealth, followed by artists, entertainers and top athletes, while highly paid bankers are seen as the least deserving. In South Korea and Japan, the sentiments are identical while in China, bankers are oddly seen as the most deserving of their wealth, even more so than entrepreneurs. Perhaps not having had a major banking crisis amidst tales of astronomical banker bonuses has something to do with this. The Vietnamese think entrepreneurs as well as money managers deserve their wealth.

And while it is not the case that Asians do not care about inequality, they are far more accepting of huge pay gaps than Westerners. Only 13 per cent of Japanese and South Koreans and 14 per cent of Vietnamese feel it is 'inappropriate' for managers to earn a hundred times more than their employees as they do not work so much longer and harder, in comparison to 63 per cent in Germany, 46 per cent in France and 39 per cent of Americans who feel this way. Again, the Chinese here are interestingly closer to Westerners in attitude with 57 per cent saying it is inappropriate for managers to earn a hundred times more than their employees.

While age has an impact on views of the wealthy in the West, with young Americans being far more critical of the rich than older people while the opposite is the case in Italy, it does not have much of an impact on attitudes in Asia. From a gender point of view, while the desire to be rich is generally stronger among Western, Chinese and Japanese males, it is equally strong among both genders in South Korea, while in Vietnam more women are keen on becoming rich than men.

African attitudes to wealth and inequality are also different from those in the West. Africa is the second-most unequal continent, just behind South America, with the top 10 per cent taking half of all the income.[3] Many have often wondered why this is accepted by Africans, especially considering the huge levels of poverty there. A study investigated attitudes in sixteen African countries where people were asked to specify on a ten-point scale their preference with respect to the statement 'Incomes should be made more equal' contrasted with the statement 'We need larger income differences as incentives for individual effort.'[4] Answers to these questions traditionally reveal opinions on whether inequality in a society should be welcomed or not.

While the responses naturally varied somewhat between African nations, the study found that 'across all self-identified class categories, African respondents in 16 African states, representative of all the regions of the continent, are on average considerably more tolerant of inequality than respondents from 43 comparable developing countries'. Africans are not just more tolerant of inequalities than Westerners but than many others in the global South. This was attributed to attitudes towards the wealthy, an aspirational optimism, and the strong role of religion on the continent.

Historically, tolerance for inequalities can be traced back to the pre-colonial era when African monarchs and traditional rulers enjoyed far greater wealth than the rest of society, as was the case everywhere else in the world at the time. It was, however, usually considered a ruler's duty to take care of their people, which most did as best they could. However, rather than a large middle-class emerging in post-colonial Africa to fundamentally transform this status quo as happened in the West and elsewhere, the so-called Big Man emerged to retain the financial dominance of rulers past.

The Big Man was able to concentrate enormous wealth in his hands, usually thanks to involvement in politics via patronage, and rent-seeking. With very little private capital available at the time of independence in the 1960s, politics was usually the only avenue to laying your hands on that first million for Africa's would-be Rockefellers. So, politics was where they went. Concentrating *both* political and financial power in their hands meant Big Men basically ran the show from start to finish. They legitimised their newfound (usually stolen) wealth by being generous with it, fulfilling the obligations to take care of others the traditional rulers of old had carried out. Big Men became walking charities to ensure the loyalty and dependence of mostly poor populations.

Unlike the Westerner, the statistical African has a very small income, lives in a society where jobs are rare, access to credit highly limited and decent education and healthcare have to be paid for as what the state provides is usually very rudimentary. Most Africans are thus constantly in need of money, a reality the wealthy are well aware of and exploit to their advantage. Their strategic generosity, which is sometimes combined with a genuinely giving nature, persists to date and is crucial in maintaining the status quo in African societies. If people feel they or their children can personally benefit from your wealth, they are less inclined to resent you or see you as undeserving.

In addition to this, religion encourages a simultaneous optimism and fatalism in African worldviews. In stark contrast to Westerners, 90 per cent of Africans consider religion important to their lives, whether they're Christian, Muslim or practise traditional African faiths. The popular belief is thus that those who have attained what so many others want – wealth – obviously have God (or the gods) on their side. Since supernatural forces are ultimately in charge of the world it is simply not possible for people to become wealthy if they are not *favoured*. And if they are favoured, there's really nothing anyone can do to change their destiny, so envying the rich is pointless. Despite having so much more, Westerners are far more envious of wealth and the wealthy than Africans.

The African view that the rich too are ultimately at the mercy of higher forces like all the rest of us humanises them in people's eyes. In the West, 'the rich' are often discussed like some alien group fundamentally different from the rest of us.

When a very wealthy person dies in Nigeria, people inevitably make comments on how money can't save you once God decides your time is up. Africans see the rich as both powerful and powerless while Westerners only see them as powerful. This creates very different feelings towards them. It is not that there are no Africans who complain about inequalities and economic discrimination, more than a few do, but we're talking here about popular sentiments which are what ultimately drive all societies.

In return for being generous, wealthy Africans are rewarded with popularity and respect. Rather than view them negatively, as is often the case in the West, the tendency is to try to get as close to them as possible, to be in their good books. People can complain about the corruption of the wealthy all they want but of what help are their complaints when money is needed to pay for a hospital bill or the children's school fees? At that moment, which is a very common moment in the lives of most Africans, the Big Man, or today occasionally Big Woman, is far more helpful than the criticiser of corruption.

Africans tend not to view wealth as an end in and of itself but as an indispensable means to the ends of survival and wellbeing, both of themselves and those around them. Those financially better off inevitably have some family members who are worse off and expect help from them. Nigerians abroad send $20 billion to their family members back home every year, not because they all have a lot of money to spare but because they simply have to help out.[5] All this means money matters a lot to most Africans, even the affluent, in a way it simply doesn't to Westerners. By extension, the wealthy hold a different position in the eyes of Africans than they do in the eyes of Westerners.

When, three years into Donald Trump's presidency, a Pew Research survey showed 58 per cent of Nigerians had confidence in him to 'do the right thing' – the fourth highest total in the world after the Philippines, Israel and Kenya – Western journalists scratched their heads in confusion.[6] How could the man who referred to African states as 'shithole countries' be so popular among Kenyans and Nigerians?

I can't speak for why Kenyans liked Trump, but what Western journalists couldn't grasp was that in the eyes of many Nigerians, Trump's wealth overshadowed his behaviour. His 1987 book, *The Art of the Deal*, was a bestseller in Nigeria long before he became president, a book I remember seeing everywhere books were sold in Lagos back when I was growing up in the 1990s. Alongside religious literature, how-to-get-rich books are the biggest bestsellers in Nigeria. Aside from their spiritual side and family, wealth is what people there are interested in. It cannot be otherwise in an environment where the baseline requirement to having a decent, safe and secure existence is having quite a lot of money.

The status hierarchies people establish in their heads are built around the dimensions they consider most relevant to their everyday lives. With money being so important to the everyday life of an African, no one comes close to the wealthy in terms of status. It is not difficult to see how this fosters views of white people, considered generally wealthy, as a high-status group to be respected and admired. As well as treated nicely.

31

It would be a mistake for anyone to assume that a Nigerian acting deferentially around a white person is doing so because of a racial complex. This is sometimes the case but often not. From the regular Nigerian's point of view, it simply makes common sense to be friendly and nice to white people as they have money, so something tangible might come out of having a good relationship with them. A job, some business, you never know. But don't get it twisted; money aside, there are many spheres of life in which Nigerians consider their ways well superior to white ways.

Whites are mocked by many Nigerians and Africans generally for the laissez-faire way they raise their kids, who are seen as spoilt brats with 'no respect' for their elders. Africans feel whites get anxious and depressed way too easily. Life setbacks they would shrug off have white folk whining, popping pills and running to therapy sessions. Rich cry-babies, really. Certainly not as mentally resilient as Africans, is the general view. Weak, some will even say.

Being religious, many Africans also judge Western societies to be morally decadent places where anything goes. You'll hear people joke that it's just a matter of time before a man is able to marry a goat in the West, that's how bonkers these white people are. 'White people don't know God,' Nigerians will comment, shaking their heads in genuine pity. Growing up in Nigeria, nobody thought Western cultural norms were inherently better than Nigerian cultural norms.

Popular perceptions of whiteness in Africa are full of contradictions, as is the human way. People are perfectly capable of feeling both more than and less than others, depending on which aspect of life you are talking about. The only thing is that some aspects of life, more precisely of the world we live in, emerge as *more relevant* in shaping their relations with others. Money is such an aspect.

Westerners don't like talking about money. Nigerians talk about money all the time, with family, friends, strangers. They talk about how much money they think others have, ranging from their neighbours to those in other countries, as this is what they use to assess the position of others in the grand scheme of things. It is no secret money is also a very big deal in the Middle East, known for its ostentatious royal families and oil sheikhs, as well as in South America, the most unequal continent in the world.

Outside the West, social relations are built around the inequality of wealth and status people enjoy in their societies, not on expectations of equality. The rich are expected to have a greater say and deferring to wealth comes instinctively to most people. In the West, the rich also have more of a say than others and people know this; the difference is that many strongly believe this should *not* be the case whereas elsewhere it is far more widely accepted. It strikes many non-Westerners as common-sensical that the rich have more of a say as they are the ones able to make things happen. Progressive Westerners not liking such worldviews is not going to stop others having them or change how they affect racial dynamics, especially in tough economic times when money plays an even greater role and has more power than during boom periods when it is more easily accessible.

The middle-class progressive Western intellectuals and activists who dominate today's race debate are more comfortable discussing ideology than discussing money. Of course, they sometimes raise the issue of Western economic domination and white wealth, but usually in a rather abstract general fashion before quickly returning to the non-material sphere of ideas they feel more comfortable and dignified discussing. It is rare to hear detailed debates on who has how much and how that affects things directly.

Western intellectuals don't even like using the word 'money', they prefer to talk about 'class', which, again, sounds more dignified, more intellectual. It also suggests there is more to status systems than just money. Yes, this is sometimes true in some places. But while it may make a big difference to Brits whether wealthy X is a duke who went to Eton, or a working-class boy made good, such distinctions are less relevant to people elsewhere. What matters is how much money you have. Not because people are shallow and simple-minded but because that is what really decides how much you can make happen.

One of the consequences of the disproportionate influence of middle-class voices in the race debate (and not only in the race debate, of course) is that their (our) preoccupation with language and ideas often obscures the stuff that matters more to most people in the world, *especially* those they (we) try to speak on behalf of.

Most people in this world are preoccupied with material issues, trying to escape financial lack or ensuring their children escape it. Consequently, they orient themselves towards the individuals and groups they perceive as having what they're looking for. As the South African kids in the study cited earlier rightly intuited, nothing determines group status as significantly as collective wealth in this capitalist world we inhabit. Other factors doubtless play a role, but none have as much power to influence events, environments and people. How does this manifest in everyday situations that link to race? As our world system is organised into nations, people get their first taste of this in that place where the national ends and the international begins: the border.

3

Visa power

Few issues bring race to the fore as strongly as immigration. In recent years, major events like the 2015 migrant crisis, Brexit, Trump's election, an increase in illegal border crossings and the rise of right-wing populism in Europe have kept immigration in the news. The issue is going nowhere and will be a matter of even greater debate and concern in the coming years. This is down to the simple fact that some parts of the world are attracting more migrants than others and that trend is only likely to intensify.

The reason race inevitably crops up when immigration is discussed is because the general direction of migration today is from the poorer global South to the rich North – eight of the top ten destination countries are thus white-majority nations.[1] The US heads the list as it has for the past half-century, Germany is in second place and Britain in fifth. Meanwhile, eight of the top ten source countries of migration are non-white nations, the likes of India, Mexico and Bangladesh providing some of the highest numbers.

While it is important to remember there are many (white) Europeans migrating within the EU and Asians migrating to other Asian countries, there are certainly more non-white people moving to white-majority nations today than vice versa. This racial dynamic lies at the root of the volatile emotions surrounding today's immigration debate. Whenever white Westerners start questioning levels of immigration to their countries, some racial minorities in those societies interpret this as a rejection of people like them. As proof they too, even if born in the Western countries they live in, are not really wanted by their white neighbours. I have experienced this feeling and it can be as real as any feeling can get, making it difficult to approach the immigration question in any remotely objective manner.

The dynamics of the immigration debate would be very different if there were as many Brits and Swedes relocating to Nigeria and Pakistan today as the other way round. A more racially balanced migration equation would foster a less emotionally volatile atmosphere for discussions around the issue of immigration, without any group interpreting this or that argument as specifically targeted at people like them.

As it stands, we live in a world in which millions of people of colour apply for visas to Western countries every year, either to visit, study or work, often hoping to prolong their stay if they can. Britain alone received 3.3 million visa applications in 2019, before Covid disrupted global travel in both 2020 and 2021.[2] The application process typically involves people from Africa, Asia and elsewhere in the global South having to jump through a significant number of hoops and usually ends with a (white) Westerner making a decision with the power to affect their life chances. Getting a visa enabling you to study at a Western university, for instance, opens doors to career opportunities in many parts of the world.

Even if no one is unpleasant or condescending towards applicants of colour during the tedious application process, they cannot but feel the brunt of the ongoing power dynamic and what it says about today's global hierarchy of nations. A nation's status in this hierarchy can be inferred from the power of its passport. The Global Passport Power Rank measures how many countries in the world each national passport enables you to visit without the need to apply for a visa in advance. In 2022, a United Arab Emirates passport was ranked the most powerful in the world, enabling you visa-free or visa-on-arrival travel to 176 countries.[3] Everyone wants a piece of that oil money.

In a video that did the social media rounds that year, Tory MP Bill Wiggin could be observed complaining to Prime Minister Boris Johnson that Qatari citizens hadn't yet been granted visa-free access to the UK. 'These are very wealthy people who are unlikely to stay and yet despite promising we'd give them visa-free access, it isn't happening ... And the only people who are turning up turn up in rubber boats. Why can't we get the *right people* through our immigration system instead of the wrong ones?', Wiggin wanted to know.

Rich brown people good, poor ones, not so much. Such moments are sorely needed in our race debate as they are more revealing than the encyclopaedias of disingenuous claptrap we usually get from politicians. Indeed, the UK has since added Qatar to its list of visa-exempt nations.

The most powerful passports in the world are those of rich nations, irrespective the skin colour of their inhabitants. You can travel to 173 countries hassle-free if you have a German, French or South Korean passport, to 171 if you have a British or Japanese passport and to 170 if you are a citizen of Canada or Singapore. However, as *most* rich nations are white-majority nations, we live in a world in which most Europeans can go pretty much wherever they want at the drop of a hat and count on being welcomed with open arms. Not simply because they are white but because they are citizens of wealthy nations and thus presumed affluent. Meanwhile, the lower ranking of the passport power index is dominated by poor nations which often tend to be black- or brown-majority nations.

You *must* get a visa to be able travel to 145 countries if you hold a Nigerian passport, to 150 countries if you hold a Bangladeshi passport, and to 154 countries if you hold a Pakistani passport. The fact most countries – 115 – still require holders of Chinese passports to apply for visas is because the Chinese are not yet a highly affluent nation in *per capita* terms, as discussed earlier. There are still many poor Chinese migrants, so the world does not yet look too favourably on the Chinese passport despite the country's overall economic superpower status. For a population their size, the Chinese have not yet amassed enough collective wealth to be global nobility.

Even if things continue to go as fantastically for their country as they have in recent decades, it is expected to take until 2050 before the *proportion* of Chinese citizens who are in that 'global middle-class' we talked about – namely people with monthly incomes above $1k – reaches Western levels.[4]

By then you can bet many more countries will be offering the Chinese visa-free travel. If by some economic miracle, Nigeria became rich in per capita terms tomorrow, I suspect many countries would review their visa requirements and suddenly discover a newfound fondness for Nigerians as well. That is the way of our world.

Even high-status individuals holding low-status passports can sometimes feel the brunt of the passport hierarchy. In a much-commented-upon interview with *The Atlantic* magazine a few years ago, the Nigerian writer Chimamanda Adichie, probably Africa's best-known contemporary author, recalled her experience at a Paris airport *en route* to that interview.[5] According to her account, on presenting her Nigerian passport to a (white) French airport official, the latter brusquely demanded to know why she was in France considering she had a Schengen visa originally issued for Spain. She explained she had just visited Spain and pointed out that a Schengen visa granted automatic entry to France as well. The Frenchman then demanded to see her return ticket to Nigeria, which she duly produced.

Despite all being in order, he kept her waiting a good while (half an hour), letting through other arrivals while ignoring her queries as to what the problem was. He finally waved her through without a word. 'For me, it was a power play. What he was saying is, *"You're not welcome here",'* Adichie told *The Atlantic*. 'He didn't have a reason for that because I had everything I needed to have as a person coming from a country that doesn't have resources, which means we are seen as people who will stay on in countries like this,' she added.

Adichie's account is revealing because it highlights how the global order, reflected in the passport hierarchy, starts impacting people's experiences of this world as soon as they leave their shores, and can shrug its shoulders at whatever personal status they may enjoy back home. This is a source of great frustration both to high achievers with 'weak' passports and to their fellow citizens who often interpret such situations as an affront. Our national treasure, treated like a nobody by a white airport official, how dare they? Many will attribute such situations to racism, and this cannot be ruled out a priori. But Adichie herself rightly recognised that 'as a person coming from a country that doesn't have resources . . . *we [Nigerians] are seen as people who will stay on in countries like this.*'

The default practice at today's international borders is for rich-nation citizens to be treated respectfully, their country's status in the global order acknowledged by the speed with which they breeze by passport controls. Poor-nation citizens, on the other hand, are often viewed suspiciously by rich-nation border officials who suspect they will be up to all sorts of devices to remain in their country.

Considering skin colour often coincides with citizenship of a rich state (as in the case of whites) and of a poor state (as in the case of blacks) race thus intersects with nationality to command respect or disrespect in such situations. In this way, the international border constantly reminds us *who is who* in the global order. The reality of course is that many citizens of poor countries *would* happily swap their home turf for France or some other rich nation.

A 2018 Gallup poll revealed 15 per cent of the world's adult population – or 750 million people – would migrate if they could, with the highest numbers expressing this desire predictably located in the poorer nations of the global South.[6] In some of the poorest nations like Liberia, Sierra Leone or Haiti, two-thirds of the population said they would migrate if they could, hardly surprising considering how difficult life can be amidst such acute scarcity. Their preferred destinations were, of course, rich nations.

A Pew Research poll conducted that same year confirmed this trend, with 54 per cent of Kenyans and 75 per cent of Ghanaians saying they would emigrate if they had the means and opportunity to do so, likewise preferably to a rich country.[7] Because the economic situation is rapidly deteriorating in my homeland, in 2021, seven out of ten Nigerians said they would leave the country if given the opportunity.[8] This is now a continental trend. A 2022 survey of Africans aged eighteen to twenty-four showed over half – 52 per cent – were considering emigrating within the next three years, citing 'economic reasons' as their chief motivation.[9] To be clear, some of them want to move to another more prosperous African country rather than outside the continent, but others cite Europe and North America as the most appealing destinations.

Everything points towards an increasing number of Africans wanting to migrate to the West in the coming years due to the combination of rapid population growth and sluggish economic development. Which is one of the reasons I say the immigration debate will only intensify in the coming years.

Not only is Africa's population expected to double to 2.5 billion by 2050, it is also the youngest continent, with 60 per cent of the population under the age of twenty-five.[10] On average, 11 million young people join the African labour market each year, yet the continent generates only 3.7 million jobs annually.[11] This in a region that already has 500 million people living in extreme poverty and is, like others, currently struggling with a cost-of-living crisis and general economic downturn.[12] There are many other countries in South Asia and the Middle East that are also producing poverty and unemployment at an alarming rate.

Clearly, these are trends rich-nation immigration policymakers are not simply going to ignore. The Western progressives who dream of a borderless world simply have no clue how incredibly difficult everyday life can be in so many parts of the world. The reality is that if a country like Britain waived visa requirements for all nationals today, there'd be ten million people here next week. And the week after that. Only those who have never lived in a country with mass poverty could possibly think otherwise.

The affluence of Western societies means they are attractive destinations not just for the direct economic opportunities they offer but also for the humane environments their wealth has enabled them to create. Nowhere in the world are human rights taken as seriously as in the West, as evidenced in the UN's Universal Human Rights Index.[13] It is no coincidence that when people flee conflicts in other parts of the world, many would, if given the choice, prefer to seek refuge in a Western country than elsewhere.

One of the main arguments of those who protested Priti Patel's plans to relocate asylum seekers in the UK to Rwanda was that their human rights would not be protected there as well as they would here in Britain. Even though Rwanda is one of Africa's best-organised states, it is difficult to dispute this particular argument. The reality is that most governments in the world are not terribly concerned with human rights. What does this have to do with wealth? you may enquire. A lot.

In theory, everyone in the world has inalienable human rights. In practice, you have as many rights as your government is able to guarantee you at home and enforce abroad. It is easier to enforce such rights both domestically and internationally when a state has the resources to build well-functioning legal systems with a sufficient number of courts, well-resourced ombudsmen, impartial judges and the whole complex bureaucratic machinery needed for the legal process to run.

Britain's Ministry of Justice alone has a budget[14] equivalent to two-thirds of the entire *national* budget of Tanzania,[15] a country similar in population to the UK. Not to mention the plethora of well-funded NGOs participating in its legal system. Countries with scant resources can rarely afford more than a bare-bones justice system incapable of realistically protecting people's human rights even if their governments had every motivation to do so. How can you hope for fair trials and prisoners to be fed decently and provided with healthcare in countries where even law-abiding citizens don't have enough to eat and die of the simplest diseases? Nothing comes free in this world, including human rights. Most nations simply lack the wherewithal to guarantee them.

Of course, thanks to regular news stories about illegal migrant crossings, the (white) Western public is aware that many black and brown people risk their lives every day trying to get into their countries. It's not difficult to imagine that for many, this is clear evidence of how much better their societies are than others. After all, *they* want to come and live *here*, usually not the other way round. This can lead to superiority complexes and condescending behaviour towards people of colour.

Which is why some of us racial minorities in the West try to downplay the attractiveness of its societies and are in fact constantly slaying them for this or that deficiency. Those who make this a practice believe white folk are already too full of themselves and feel better than us as it is, if anything they need to be brought down a peg or two. Otherwise, they'll always position themselves above us. There's a solid logic to this stance, considering betterthanism is not that rare an attitude in Westerners, including those who like to think themselves very progressive (more on them later).

We also shouldn't dance around the fact that there remains more than a fair bit of racism in the Western world. A 2022 survey of black people in Europe showed nearly half – 45 per cent – saying they had experienced racist discrimination in the last five years, up from 39 per cent in 2016.[16] The figure stood at 61 per cent and 66 per cent in Denmark and Finland, nations usually associated with tolerance, while three-in-four black respondents in Austria and Germany – 76 per cent and 77 per cent – reported experiencing racist discrimination. The fact that African migrants in Europe tolerate incidents of white racism is sad evidence of just how badly their own societies and governments have failed them.

A 2019 UN study of 1,970 migrants from thirty-nine African countries in thirteen European nations, all of whom admitted they had arrived in Europe through 'irregular' means and *not* for asylum or protection-related reasons, showed 93 per cent saying they would make the journey again, despite facing often life-threatening danger.[17] 'The idea to try and reduce the weight of migration is to look at the causes. It is . . . the governing policies that entrench people in poverty, that don't develop anything. Schools that don't exist, failing health [systems] and corruption, repression. That pushes people to emigrate,' said one respondent.

Ultimately, Western countries remain attractive migrant destinations for their economic opportunities as well as their reputations for respecting human rights and being generally well-run societies where you can pursue your life aspirations in relative safety and comfort compared to many places elsewhere. Of course, there are some rich nations like the Persian Gulf states of Kuwait, Qatar, Saudi Arabia et al that are not very big on human rights, yet attract a lot of immigration for purely economic reasons. Which just shows how important it is for people to be where they can make a good living, *even if* their freedoms are restricted there.

What national affluence offers, though, is the practical potential to realistically protect human rights – potential Western nations tend to make use of. What all this means for big-picture race dynamics is that predominantly white governments and immigration authorities wield gatekeeping control over some of the best and most humane living conditions in the world today, a dynamic entrenching the existing global and racial order.

There are certainly some good arguments against maintaining a twenty-first-century immigration system de facto based on birthright privileges reminiscent of the feudal era. The geographical lottery of birth is perhaps the cruellest fate of all today. We can also choose to remind white people of the fact that there was a period in history when they migrated all over the world in search of opportunities, especially to the global South, despite its indigenous populations being less than thrilled with their presence. And they didn't just migrate and politely 'assimilate', they set up settler colonies imposing white rule everywhere from South Africa to Australia. *Those* migrants didn't apply for no visas. But while bringing up such arguments may give us some moral satisfaction and win the applause of those who insist any discussion of the world today that doesn't recall colonialism et al is 'ahistorical', they're unlikely to change anything in the sphere of practical realities.

Moreover, the fact most Westerners believe they should have immigration policies favouring their interests is not because they are inherently more egoistic than others. Ipsos MORI compiles a yearly Nativism Index based on people's agreement or disagreement with the following three statements: 'Our country would be stronger if we stopped immigration.' 'When jobs are scarce, employers should prioritise hiring people of this country over immigrants.' 'Immigrants take jobs away from "real" nationals.'[18] In its 2021 survey, people in countries like Turkey, Malaysia, Colombia, Argentina, South Africa and Mexico were *more likely* to agree with these statements than were Americans, Australians, Germans, Brits or Canadians.

So, despite the real racism that still exists in the West, the root of the border problem and its effect on the racial hierarchy is less to be found in a unique nativism of whites than in the fact many of the countries people currently find attractive to move to happen to be white-majority nations. This gives white folk way too much leverage in the immigration equation, ultimately perpetuating a dynamic that entrenches the existing racial hierarchy and sustains white status. To change this dynamic would require changing the fundamentals of that equation. It would, in short, require the building of successful nations elsewhere that millions of people want to emigrate to.

4

Respect

Today's race debate revolves around how people not white are treated in the West, be they recent immigrants or descendants of those who came long ago. Few things matter as much to people as the feeling they're treated with respect in their everyday lives. When people feel disrespected, they can become angry and resentful. Feelings of disrespect are the most underappreciated emotions in race relations. As Alicia Garza, the African American co-founder of BLM put it: 'Black Lives Matter is not just concerned with what happens in policing. The disregard, disrespect, and lack of dignity for black life transcends through the fabric of our society.'[1]

This feeling of disrespect is discernible in black and other racial minority complaints about everything from institutional bias to microaggressions. Being treated respectfully matters to people because it feels nice and boosts self-esteem but also because it sends a message others note. In Western societies where multiple racial and ethnic groups often share a space, people also pay attention to whether people *like them* are treated respectfully or not.

If a white British boss in a London office makes disparaging remarks about Africa to a Nigerian employee, the Kenyans there will worry they too could soon be on the receiving end of similar comments. Minorities everywhere are mindful of such incidents as they are more anxious about their place in society than members of majority groups. This is down to the psychological asymmetry that characterises majority–minority interactions in various cultures, irrespective of whether the dividing lines are racial, ethnic or religious. In the Middle East, the Shia–Sunni religious divide is often key; where the one is the majority, the other worry about their status in the country. The mere awareness there are more of *them* than there are of *us* produces a defence mechanism deeply embedded in our tribal brains.

While a boss making disparaging remarks about an employee's continent is an easy case to judge disrespectful, what constitutes respectful treatment is subjective and boils down to how people believe others *should* behave towards them. Culture, psychology and occupational status play a role. In Nigeria, it's considered disrespectful to address someone ten years older than you by their first name as you're expected to demonstrate deference towards your seniors in language and manner. In Britain, twenty-year-olds speak to fifty-year-olds like they were equals and no one thinks much of it. It's easy to see potential misunderstandings if the fifty-year-old Nigerian moves to London and interprets the casual manner a young white Briton adopts with him as stemming from the fact he is black rather than because age hierarchies mean little here.

Some people are quicker to perceive slight due to personal insecurities that usually stem from way back in their childhood. We all know people you need to walk on eggshells around as even the slightest offhand remark can offend them. As for the role of occupational status, people who are highly educated and considered very good at their jobs tend to expect more respect than is granted others because they feel they have 'earned' it. They can get quite touchy if they feel they are not being treated as respectfully as they think they should be. Another factor which affects perceptions of respectful treatment is that people from groups who feel generally looked down on can sometimes perceive disrespect where it doesn't exist because that is what they *expect*. Such anticipation of disrespect can lead to classic confirmation bias. These caveats aside, however, feelings of disrespect are clearly affecting race relations in the West today.

Like equality, perceptions of respect are comparative. When people say they want to be equal, one may ask: equal to who? When they say they want to be treated respectfully, one may also ask: so, treated like who? The answer in this case is that racial minorities want to be treated *as respectfully* as they feel white people are treated.

They don't just want to be spared disparaging remarks, they want to be noticed, not 'marginalised'. They want to feel their opinions matter. It is one thing to be politely allowed to have your say, quite another to feel what you say carries actual weight with your listeners. People can usually figure out if this is the case or not, especially in environments like the workplace where they can see if higher-ups are actually acting on their proposals and suggestions.

Of course, there are many white Americans, Brits and Swedes who will feel their opinions are regularly ignored at work and elsewhere as well, but being the majority in their societies, they won't attribute this to their skin colour but to something else, usually their personal status or others simply being assholes. So, what do those who today feel disrespected by white people because of their skin colour feel can rectify the situation? 'Education' is a very popular answer.

Initiatives from Black History Month to calls for the 'decolonisation' of Western education are based on the premise that respect for black people and other minorities in the West can be educated into white people by familiarising them with the great writers, philosophers and scientists to have emerged from those groups as well as the histories of how their ancestors oppressed and exploited those groups.

Education is a very appealing answer as it is one that appears to propose a solution within relatively easy reach. Teach white kids what their ancestors did in India and Africa and about accomplished pre-colonial African states like the Bini Empire in today's Nigeria or Timbuktu in today's Mali and their mindsets will shift. The problem is that when it comes to *mass sentiment*, which is what affects the lives of everyday minorities in the West, human psychology suggests something different.

Social psychology has spent the last century trying to figure out what drives how people treat other people. It has emerged that there are two central dimensions around which people orient themselves towards other individuals and groups: their perceived *warmth* and *competence*.[2] The notion of warmth in this context involves friendliness, trustworthiness, likeability and sincerity. They combine moral evaluations (sincerity,

52

trustworthiness) with assumptions of pro- or antisocial traits. People look for signs of these to gauge the *intentions* others have towards them: Friend or foe? People we can feel safe around or not? Fun to interact with or not?

How people read your intentions towards them shapes how they interpret what you say and do. Let me give an example. Chinua Achebe, a Nigerian widely considered one of the greatest writers of the twentieth century and often referred to as the 'grandfather of African literature', wrote this about his homeland in his book *The Trouble with Nigeria*:

> One of the commonest manifestations of underdevelopment is a tendency among the ruling elite to live in a world of make-believe and unrealistic expectations. This is the *cargo cult* mentality that anthropologists sometimes speak about – a belief by backward people that someday without any exertion whatsoever on their own part, a fairy ship will dock in their harbour laden with every goody they have always dreamed of possessing. Listen to Nigerian leaders and you will frequently hear the phrase 'this great country of ours'. Nigeria is not a great country. It is one of the most disorderly nations in the world. It is one of the most corrupt, insensitive, inefficient places under the sun. It is one of the most expensive countries and one of those that give least value for money. It is dirty, callous, noisy, ostentatious, dishonest and vulgar. In short, it is among the most unpleasant places on earth!

Achebe's depiction of Nigeria was widely discussed when his book came out in the 1980s and is still cited by Nigerians to date. Many agreed with much of the description, no one was offended by it. Now imagine if a famous white writer had written those words. Same words, commas in exact same places. The response would have been very different. Many Nigerians would have felt offended, disrespected. The white author would be assumed to have *negative intentions* towards Nigerians, to be bent on portraying us badly, likely due to racism. It of course never crossed anyone's mind to assume any such thing with Achebe and he remains as revered in Nigeria today as he was back then. What is said or done is less important than who is doing the saying and doing. In-group members are generally judged with a different set of rules than out-group members who are separated into friend or foe camps. The Americans are fine with Britain having nuclear weapons but don't want Iran to have them. Same weapons, only difference is in the intentions they assign the actors. How people read your intentions determines to a large extent how they will judge your actions.

As for the competence dimension, it includes traits like efficiency, intelligence, skill and confidence. People assess these qualities in others to identify those who have the capacity to *implement their intentions* and must thus be reckoned with. Those they need to factor into their life plans, whether they want to or not. To be able gauge the intentions of others and their abilities to implement those intentions, people resort to stereotypes.

Studies on how various groups are perceived, ranging from age and gender groups to ethnic, racial and national groups, have led to psychologists developing a Stereotype Content Model (SCM). This reveals how stereotypes share *common content* across cultures. Whether it's Nigerians stereotyping the ethnic groups in their society or Americans stereotyping the racial groups in theirs, common patterns emerge. They revolve around warmth and competence perceptions and drive common attitudes towards groups.

Stereotypes of others are never all-good or all-bad but a mix of perceptions on various dimensions of warmth and competence. The saying that the Germans love the Italians but don't admire them while the Italians admire the Germans but don't love them captures this ambivalence. When it comes to how friendly or sincere people feel other groups are, personal encounters often decide. Some will think Nigerians good friendly people, others may not. Some will say the English are cold, others will disagree, though of course certain peoples do seem to be widely stereotyped as warm and friendly, Brazilians, for instance. Their entertaining 'Samba football' and colourful carnivals certainly help with this image.

Competence perceptions, however, are more predictable because they are not random but flow from existing material structures. A group's position in these structures can predict the stereotypes about it, which can in turn predict common attitudes towards its members. Groups with the capacity to implement their intentions are considered high-status groups and stereotyped as competent while those lacking such capabilities are viewed as low-status groups and stereotyped as less competent.[3] Implementing group plans of any significant kind of course requires financial resources.

The Swiss can decide to build a nuclear power plant today and commence building tomorrow as they have the billions needed to finance such a project. If the Rwandan government takes the same decision today, it will need to first raise the necessary finance from somewhere as it does not have that kind of money. If it can't raise the money (from the likes of the Swiss), its intentions will remain intentions. Though both small nations, the Swiss have a far greater ability to make things happen.

It's not a coincidence America, Britain, Canada, China, Germany, Japan, South Korea and Singapore are all stereotyped as competent nations. We see this in 'soft power' rankings which assess how nations are perceived in spheres ranging from economic strength, quality of governance, educational systems and scientific achievements (competence perceptions) to culture and heritage, people and values (warmth perceptions).

In 2022, the US was ranked the nation with the most soft power in the world, followed by Britain, Germany, China and Japan.[4] These top five nations are also the world's five biggest economies, and all are perceived as competent nations. South Africa, Africa's wealthiest nation, was its highest-ranking on the list, in thirty-fourth position. The nations with the least soft power, usually poor nations, are generally not rated competent by others. Like the passport power index, the upper echelons of soft power rankings are dominated by affluent nations.

People equate group status with competence because most assume successful groups got to where they are thanks to some kind of collective ability or combination of abilities rather than sheer luck. Whether people believe we live in a world that is benignly meritocratic or dog-eat-dog, groups that have done well for themselves are seen as effective. The question of who is seen as competent is really the question of who is seen as *effective*. Who is where others want to be and has what others want? Considering there are no nations or peoples that would *not* like to be wealthy and successful, the world distinguishes between those who have been effective at achieving this and those who haven't.

After finishing secondary school in Nigeria in the mid-nineties, I moved to Poland, my mother's homeland. I always found it intriguing how Poles stereotyped others and why. It was clear from the beginning they considered Westerners more competent than themselves. 'We want things here to work normally, like in the West,' they would say. When the Berlin Wall collapsed after half a century of communism, Poland's GDP per capita was just a tenth that of the likes of Britain and Germany. This clearly had an impact on how Poles stereotyped those nations. More intriguingly, they didn't just consider Westerners more competent, but also the Japanese and South Koreans. The competence order was not a straightforward racial order in their minds.

Following communism's demise, major Japanese and Korean corporations like Toyota, Honda, Hyundai, Sony and Samsung shifted production lines to Poland, lured by a cheaper workforce with manufacturing experience. With these corporations came a cadre of Japanese and Korean managers who came to *teach* Poles the ways of doing things that had made them so successful. These were no poor immigrants, but bringers of capital and know-how that Poland desperately needed. It was Poles who worked for the Japanese and Koreans, not the other way round. Poles were very respectful towards *these* non-whites. Lech Wałęsa, Poland's first post-communist president, once promised he would turn his country into a 'second Japan'. The popular reaction wasn't, 'But why should we want to be like them? After all, we're white so we're better.' It was more like, 'A Japan *here*? If only!'

The Japanese were so many rungs higher up the economic hierarchy, Poles were incapable of thinking themselves better simply because they were white. Those who worked for the Japanese and Korean conglomerates would speak in awe about how hard-working and disciplined they were in comparison to Poles. To balance the equation somewhat and not feel too bad about themselves, Poles stereotyped East Asians negatively on warmth dimensions. They were apparently *too* focused on work and profit, not fun to be around, generally not particularly likeable people. Successful East Asian nations are often stereotyped as competent but cold.[5]

Successful nations and groups benefit greatly from *positive stereotypes* in the competence sphere, which reflect their status while simultaneously legitimising it. They enjoy a specific kind of virtuous circle: Succeed – Be seen as competent – Succeed even more thanks to this perception. There are probably more than a few lazy Japanese, Koreans and Germans, but you wouldn't think so listening to how people go on about their work ethic. This is how competence stereotypes help sustain material hierarchies, ensuring some are instinctively accorded more respect and opportunities than others.

Studies show members of groups deemed competent can get a 'stereotype lift' in performance because they come to believe people *like them* are indeed competent. Conversely, negative stereotypes about their group's competence can lead to people behaving in ways that reinforce these stereotypes, becoming self-fulfilling prophesies. In one fascinating study, Asian women were found to underperform on maths tests in situations in which gender was made salient (when they were primed to compare men and women), while doing better when their Asian identity was made salient, in line with stereotypes of Asians being good at maths but women not.[6]

But if Americans are stereotyped as competent, why are black Americans and some other groups of Americans often stereotyped to the contrary, one may well ask. Of all the black collectives in the world, black Americans are by far the wealthiest and highest status. Their position is reflected in the huge influence black American culture has in the world, in music, fashion, literature and ideas. The black household names in the world tend to be from America, the Oprah Winfreys, Toni Morrisons, Kanye Wests, Obamas et al.

The average global citizen can probably not even name a single Kenyan figure they are familiar with, even though there are more Kenyans than African Americans. In fact, if you say Kenya, they'll probably say Barack Obama! When I lived in Warsaw, Poles treated the black Americans there far more respectfully than they treated us Africans. They were clearly seen as higher status than us for being *Americans*.

However, *within* America, black Americans are socioeconomically disadvantaged relative to other groups and are often portrayed by both outsiders and insiders as an oppressed low-status group with virtually no say in society compared to white people. The situation is similar in Britain and other Western societies whose black populations are usually portrayed, again, by both outsiders and insiders, as being at the bottom of society, which in material terms, is indeed usually the case. This, in addition to some genuinely racist beliefs held about black folk, negatively affects perceptions of black American competence.

Simultaneously, black folk are often stereotyped positively on warmth dimensions, as outgoing, cool, fun people to be with. Blackness is often associated with the cool factor. Black artistes are helped by the stereotypes that if you're black, you're probably better at singing, rapping, dancing et al than others. That you have *soul*. There are of course also stereotypes of black people as aggressive, which are negative perceptions on the warmth dimension. Again, stereotypes are a mishmash of perceptions on various dimensions; what matters is which stereotypical dimensions have the *greatest impact* on the group's fortunes. Considering its relevance to getting ahead, the competence sphere has the largest impact on a group's fortunes.

Take Jews, for instance, another prominent minority group in the West. They are often stereotyped as disproportionately rich and influential, rendering them high-status. Much of the prejudice against Jews, including the most extreme form brought on by Hitler and his Nazis, exploited existing stereotypes of them as devilishly clever people secretly running the world. A people who had supposedly single-handedly engineered Germany's defeat in the First World War and were keeping the German nation down. You can't convince people a group they consider incompetent is secretly running the world.

But such propagandistic portrayals of Jews were effective because they have long been viewed as a very competent people. While in societies where they are minorities, they do face prejudice, it is an envious kind of prejudice. To whip up sentiments against them, the Nazis would often argue Jews were over-represented in high-status professions in Germany, ranging from academia to law. Like Asian Americans in the US today, another group seen as highly successful, Jews are often stereotyped as competent but cold.[7]

In gender stereotypes, the successful career woman is also often portrayed this way with phrases like 'iron maiden', 'ball buster' and 'ice queen'. Groups stereotyped as competent but cold are not particularly warmed to or attributed good intentions, but they are respected. People may not seek to be friends with them or go partying with them, but they want to employ them and do business with them. Because they are seen as effective.

Groups stereotyped as warm but less competent elicit sympathy or even pity if their status is linked to forces beyond their control. Ageist portrayals of older people as kind but incompetent are a good example, as are portrayals of housewives as warm, loving and generally harmless. White progressives often display pitying attitudes towards black people. They read books written by other progressives about the lasting effects of slavery, colonialism and racism, and come away with a 'poor them' attitude.

Even when pity stems from empathy and is seen as allyship, it is an attitude drenched in paternalism. It positions the pitier above as pity is always directed downwards (while envy is directed upwards). The pitier assumes a lofty position, often emphasising how *unwillingly* they occupy it to signal their moral disapproval of the order that placed them there. *Alas, I wish it weren't so that I am here above you. But don't worry, I will help. I am one of the good ones. Powerful, but good.* This is a mighty comfortable position to be in, enabling one to enjoy the benefits both of material status and perceived moral virtue.

The white saviour complex is the most famous child of this attitude, dating back to when colonialism was justified by portrayals of Africans as friendly simple-minded 'picaninnies', to quote Boris Johnson, who needed guidance. If African leaders are corrupt, white progressives will blame it on Western 'power structures' that are leading them astray or perhaps even forcing them to rob their own people, poor things. Poor-them attitudes thrive on highly asymmetrical power relations. Helpers are not needed where there are no dependents.

In contrast, those who do not see a group's low status as stemming from forces beyond its control can be contemptuous of its members' competence, dismissing them as ineffectual. Southern Nigerian stereotypes of the much poorer and less-educated northern Nigerians are rife with such portrayals. Because they live in the same country and are thus seen as subject to the same circumstances, their situation is popularly deemed a result of their ineptitude. A plethora of studies on ethnic stereotypes in Africa and Asia show successful groups are stereotyped as competent and advanced while less successful groups are stereotyped as incompetent and backward.[8]

Those who don't believe black poverty is due to forces beyond black control can thus be dismissive of black ability. However, aside from a few committed racists, few today deny the potential of *black individuals* to become great engineers, lawyers, doctors, entrepreneurs, writers or poets. White Brits didn't rush to withdraw their savings when Kwasi Kwarteng was announced Chancellor. And even during the market chaos that ensued after his 'mini-budget' announcement, no one was suggesting he wasn't competent enough to be in charge of Britain's finances *because he is black*. Dismissive attitudes towards black ability, where they do exist, are linked rather to doubts about the large-scale organisational competence required to effectively harness black resources towards building successful nations, the most relevant large-scale organisations around today.

In *this sense*, it is true not much has changed from colonial-era views of black people as lacking what it takes for effective self-government. This is visible in the plethora of 'good governance' recommendations institutions like the IMF and World Bank regularly produce for African states which are viewed as badly run and poorly organised. While there are some prosperous black-majority nations, they tend to be small Caribbean islands like Barbados or Bahamas with populations of less than half a million, or the rare African example of two-million strong Botswana. These nations are too small and too under the radar to erase stereotypes about the 1.4 billion people racialised as black today. We are of course always free to describe such stereotypes as racist, but that doesn't mean they will go away.

Because negative stereotypes of blackness today are more to do with large-scale organisational competence, emphasising *individual* black success stories, a trend visible in social media campaigns like #blackexcellence and #blackgirlmagic, cannot fundamentally shift perceptions *in this dimension*. We constantly hear of such and such being the 'first black person' to be elected X or Y, to be made CEO or to win such and such award. Showcasing black success stories matters. Obama getting elected president of the most powerful nation on earth mattered a lot. These stories do shift the dial, but they shift it too weakly to transform the overall picture. Moreover, there is an implicit downside to these black excellence stories emerging from Western societies.

To many white Westerners, the ascendance of black (and brown) individuals to high-status positions in the West simply confirms how meritocratic the societies *they* have built are, places where anyone can thrive or even become prime minister like Rishi Sunak if they're good enough. In contrast to, say, African societies widely seen as plagued by corruption, nepotism and 'tribalism', the opposite of competence-based meritocracies. To compound matters, these are views widely shared by Africans themselves. Nigerians often complain bitterly about how it is easier for a talented Nigerian with no connections to make it in the West than in Nigeria where someone's potential can often go to waste because they don't know the 'right people'.

All this helps perpetuate a stereotype of black folk as not just less competent organisationally but as people who shun meritocracies where they are in charge. Rather than the 'poor them' attitude of white progressives, many whites, certainly many conservative whites, tend more along the lines of 'they just can't seem to get their act together'.

Aside from ideology, national histories also shape stereotypical attitudes. Because of the guilt some white Westerners feel for slavery and colonialism, they're more likely to sympathise with the situation of Africans or Asians than Eastern Europeans who never had colonies and weren't major players in the slave trade. Polish opinions of black competence are encapsulated in a saying they use to emphasise their frustrations when things don't work well in their country: 'We're a hundred years behind the blacks!' they'll scoff. This is meant as a deliberate hyperbole to highlight how far Poland still has to go. When I complained about it to a fellow student, his response was: 'Sorry you feel offended, but Africa *is* behind every other continent developmentally. That's just a fact. And Africa is where you guys are in charge.'

When I'd bring up history, Poles would acknowledge Africa had been ruthlessly exploited but then go on to recall their own history. Losing their independence for 123 years from 1795 to 1918, then being invaded by Hitler in 1939 and having their capital reduced to rubble, then being abandoned by the West to half a century of Soviet communist domination which left them poorer and weaker than other European nations. 'Most of the last two hundred years were pretty crap for us too,' they'd conclude. In other words: Get over your past, you're not the only victims of history.

Following Brexit, more than five million EU nationals have obtained settled status in the UK, the bulk of them from Eastern Europe.[9] Polish has been the most common non-British nationality in Britain since 2007.[10] There are now more Eastern Europeans in Britain than black people. Many will soon acquire British citizenship and start voting in UK elections. Yet, Eastern European whiteness, which is quite distinct from its Western manifestation, is never quite factored into the race debate.

This impoverishes our understanding of popular white attitudes that exist among us and are going nowhere. Eastern

European nations are also becoming increasingly assertive in European politics, as seen throughout the Russia–Ukraine war. Following their successful economic transformations – Poland is now ranked a high-income country – their influence in shaping Europe's future, including in the attitudinal sphere, will only grow.

Moreover, even though history and political correctness mean few Westerners will say to an African's face the things Poles said to mine, that doesn't mean they're not *thinking* it. Students at Princeton University rated ten ethnic and national groups on the same eighty-four adjectives four times over the past seventy years, resulting in a coherent stereotype map at each time point.[11] Consistent with changing norms, students became increasingly more reluctant to voice out stereotypes' negative dimensions, emphasising instead positive dimensions ('they're friendly people').

However, the end result of the stereotypical map they have today rates the British high in competence and warmth; Turks lower in both competence and warmth; African Americans warmer but less competent; and Japanese, Chinese, Germans and Jews as competent but less warm.

A group stereotype evolves along with the group's objective status position. A few decades ago, the stereotype of Chineseness was of the poor Chinaman in the rice fields. That is clearly no longer the case. But contrary to what those who think teaching the histories of less successful groups can make them more respected believe, aside from a handful of Sinophiles back then, the world didn't care that China was a five-thousand-year-old civilisation once looked up to by others. People still made jokes about the proverbial Chinaman in the rice fields. Growing up in 1990s Nigeria, we didn't think much of Chineseness either – today I constantly hear Nigerians saying the Chinese will soon 'take over the world'.

How many people today know that less than a hundred years ago, Argentina was one of the wealthiest nations in the world, outgrowing the US, Canada and Australia in total and per capita income between 1900 and 1930? In 1913, it was richer than France or Germany, and almost twice as prosperous as Spain.[12] If people knew, would they care? Would it make them perceive Argentinians as just as competent as South Koreans, who used to be poor when Argentina was very rich? Unlikely. In the sphere of competence perceptions, the world doesn't care where you were in the past, it cares where you are today.

It is important to teach the histories of black people and other racial minorities in the West if only for the reason of broadening Western horizons, which can be exasperatingly myopic. Authors and thinkers from today's disadvantaged groups should be promoted as there is plenty we can all learn from each other. But we should also realise that whoever does pick up a book by a black writer or watches a documentary about black people likely already has *some respect* for black folk. Those who don't simply won't pick up that book or will change the channel when the documentary comes on. So, this is often a case of preaching to the converted. And while you can force students to read certain books if they have to do so to pass their exams, what happens once they leave university? Respect is not something you can legislate or force people to feel.

While education can temper stereotypes, it is unlikely to ever eliminate them, because stereotypes are widely acknowledged by psychologists to guide people's behaviour in ambiguous contexts. Not just white people, all people. When we say 'white people' are such and such, we are also engaging in stereotyping, and we do that all the time as I am doing in this book! By the way, those who insist on constantly portraying white people as 'imperialists' who have been exploiting and dominating everyone for centuries should realise they are strengthening perceptions of white competence. After all, it takes some doing to run the world and constantly keep a step ahead of others. Even if their actions are evaluated negatively in the moral dimension, it still leaves white people with the image of being, at worst, sinful winners. That is not the worst image to have in a world focused on results.

While it is possible for an individual to disconfirm a stereotype about *people like them*, it takes a lot more to render a stereotype completely absurd in mass sentiment, which is the only way to really kill it. Just as it would take a lot to convince the world today that the Japanese and Germans are lazy and incompetent, so it would take a lot to change stereotypes about some groups deemed incompetent in this or that sphere today. You cannot change a social reality without acknowledging what drives it.

We all want to be treated respectfully. We all want to be treated as individuals, not depersonalised as members of this or that group. I know all too well what it's like to be stereotyped negatively from my years in Poland. But it is worth facing the fact that, like it or not, people of all skin colours *will* continue to make snap judgements of other groups based on their perceived competence, which will often be based on their status, which in turn will be chiefly based on how well they are doing economically.

Successful groups will be respected, those seen as not successful will at best be sympathised with. What you want is for your group to be stereotyped as positively as possible in the competence sphere. To do that requires being successful in collective, not just individual, terms. For better or worse, the road to group respect lies in economics, not in history or education.

5

How Western academia sustains white status

Another thing strongly associated with competence is knowledge. How people know what they know about the world and who they know it from always reveals a lot about the order of the day. I moved to the UK in 2015 and have since taught politics at the University of Sheffield and for the past two years at the University of York. I've had a great time and find it difficult to think of a more interesting way to spend one's days than discussing ideas with young people and learning how they perceive the world. It is an educative experience and I've learnt way more than I've taught. I've never felt disadvantaged by my skin colour. Nevertheless, I have little doubt Western academia is a central upholder of white status in the world, which by default makes it a sustainer of the existing racial order.

This may sound counterintuitive to some, considering one of the most popular buzzwords of Western academia in recent years is 'decolonisation', and Western universities are increasingly seen as bastions of woke activism rather than status quo maintainers. There's no doubt Western academia is currently undergoing insurgencies aimed at toppling the existing order. It is now very fashionable in academic circles to be seen as 'speaking truth to power', which often boils down to claiming that pretty much everything presented to us as facts by 'Western education' are biased 'narratives' cooked up by the powerful to entrench their domination. The powerful being white Westerners broadly, and white males in particular.

You will thus hear a lot of talk in universities these days about the need to 'decentre whiteness' from knowledge production and pretty much everything else. Arguments in this direction invariably elicit many nods and few questions. They are often made or at least supported by top scholars with plenty of prestige and power in academia. The cleverest proponents of these views are very adept at moralising the discourse ('it's about justice') and deploying irony, so it is not always easy for less influential scholars to feel confident enough to risk a withering rebuke by challenging the views of those higher up the academic pecking order. Safer to nod along.

As a result, one in three UK academics who identify as centre-right regularly self-censor by refraining from airing their views at work. The same is true for one in six academics who identify as centre-left.[1] This is not a healthy atmosphere. Universities should be places where people feel free to air their views, so you can hear all kinds of perspectives on the same subject and think, 'Wow, I never thought about it *that way* before.'

They should not be places where ideas can become dominant not because they have effectively handled scrutiny but because people are wary of scrutinising them for fear of their intentions being questioned ('Yeah, well, he *would* say that, wouldn't he, after all he's a . . . '). Universities should not be places where you can walk into a room and predict what pretty much everyone in it will say on certain issues. This either means there's incredible groupthink going on or many are simply pretending to think a certain way. Either way, it's a problem.

Other academics aside, another major source of conformist pressure is social media. And I'm not just talking about the flogged issue of cancel culture. We used to live in a world where twenty-year-olds tried to impress forty-year-olds because their careers depended on the latter. Today, we live in a world where forty-year-olds try to impress twenty-year-olds because the young dominate social media and can boost your career prospects by making you popular online.

The trend of academics joining other commentators to spit fire on Twitter, like for instance when the Queen died, is largely a result of this dynamic. If you figure out what or who the young don't like and bash that or them, you're guaranteed attention, an obviously valuable commodity for an intellectual. Never have the young wielded as much influence as they do today, not as individuals but as an audience.

Furthermore, at the end of the day, universities are a business and the young their customer base. Those in charge of running universities are strongly motivated to please this customer base as tuition fees usually constitute the bulk of university incomes. They therefore pay close attention to popular opinion among the young and strive to show they're on the same page. The students who do care a lot about race issues (not all do by any means) are very vocal in their antiracist declarations, so university authorities will endorse pretty much any slogans they come up with and would be aghast at any suggestion they are somehow furthering a racial order.

The problem with all this is that you can perpetuate an order without consciously striving to. For the crux of the hierarchy in knowledge production today lies not in the individual behaviours of students, academics or even university authorities but in the overarching status structure of global academia.

While scholars and organised centres of learning have existed for centuries around the world, it is not until the post-Second World War era that we can begin to speak of a standardised global university system per se. This was largely down to the attainment of independence by dozens of nations in Africa and Asia who, now in charge of their own finances, often set about building universities with gusto to equip their young with the knowledge to compete in a global economy. During the colonial era, their white rulers were rarely interested in building many universities on their lands. A few here and there to create a local cadre capable of helping administer the colony, but they certainly didn't want *too many* educated natives.

From the 1950s onwards, nations in Asia and Africa built thousands of new universities employing hundreds of thousands of scholars who joined an emerging global academic community. For some time, this heralded a significantly equalising moment in history. But only for some time. The universities of the world's new superpower – America – along with those of its old superpower – Britain – soon emerged as *the* most influential centres of knowledge production. In the so-called Francophone world, made up of former French colonies, French universities often became the go-to places for knowledge. In the communist

73

world, Russian universities came to play a major role in knowledge dissemination with Moscow emerging as a Mecca for communist thinkers. Needless to say, these were all white-run universities.

Today, Western universities enjoy a credibility and prestige universities elsewhere struggle to compete with. In the 2022 edition of the oft-referenced QS World University Rankings, which evaluates universities' reputations among academics and employers among others, sixteen of the top twenty universities in the world were located in the West, mostly in America and Britain.[2] For a broader picture, thirty-seven of the top fifty universities were in Western countries.

All the non-Western universities that made the top fifty ranking were in East Asia – in China, Japan and Singapore. The highest-ranked African university – the University of Cape Town in South Africa – came in at 226th. A Chinese ranking of the world's best universities produced similar results to the QS version, so this is not just down to the 'Western bias' of such rankings, which do indeed tend to be compiled by Western institutions.[3]

It is no coincidence the best universities in the world tend to be in the richest nations of the world, including the East Asian entries. It is likewise no coincidence that the highest-ranked black-run university is in South Africa, the continent's richest and best-developed country. As with most other institutions, it is very difficult to build a world-class version without significant resources. Money matters in academia as much as anywhere else. Harvard University has more in its endowment fund than the Nigerian state in foreign reserves.[4] The University of York, where I currently work, wielded a budget of £421 million in 2021.[5] The entire education budget of Nigeria that year, including spending on all levels from primary schools to universities (which are often state-run), amounted to the equivalent of £1.2 billion.[6] The wealthiest British universities like Oxford and Cambridge have annual budgets exceeding £2 billion. A single Western university can often wield a budget larger than all the universities in a global South nation put together.

As I mentioned earlier, after independence many post-colonial states made vigorous attempts at building world-class universities. Nigerian academia flourished during the oil-boom years of the 1970s when cash was flush in the country, employing academics from all over the globe and nourishing local talents like Wole Soyinka, the first black African to win the Nobel prize for literature, among many others. When my parents moved to Nigeria in 1970, they lived on a university campus for a while and my mother, who had been a journalist in Poland, would often recall she never met so many interesting minds in her life. Unfortunately, the economic crises of the 1980s, which led to drastic cuts in spending on education, dealt Nigerian universities body blows from which they have yet to recover.

Facing worsening pay and work conditions, many of Nigeria's brightest academics starting emigrating in the 1980s, mostly to research and teach in well-resourced Western universities. This became a common pattern in the post-colonial world as many states grappled with economic crises of all sorts after the first decades of independence, subsequently suffering 'brain drains' in all professions. It is a pattern that persists today as the paying power, prestige and comfortable working environment of Western universities means they continue to draw some of the brightest scholars from around the world, including many from the global South, who end up contributing to Western intellectual output. This despite the fact evidence shows there is discrimination in Western university hiring practices.

One study on UK university hiring patterns found that black candidates and those of Asian descent needed to make anything from 30 to 60 per cent *more* job applications than white Britons to get the same number of interviews the latter did.[7] In US academia, where non-white scholars have a stronger position than in the UK, black, Hispanic and multiracial faculty members remain under-represented in faculty ranks.[8] The fact that so many scholars from around the world continue to seek work in Western universities despite this only goes to show the power of their pull. And the lack of viable alternatives elsewhere. Many African scholars in the West today would be happier educating the next generation of Kenyans and Nigerians rather than the next generation of Britons and Americans. The higher education needs in Africa are far greater than in the West due to its rapid population growth. The problem is with the financial condition of universities there.

Meanwhile, the pulling power Western universities enjoy means there's never a shortage of foreign students looking to hand them their money. And education is big money, globally a $6 trillion industry.[9] Over five million students study abroad each year and Western universities get most of the action. Seven of the ten most popular destinations for foreign students in 2020 were Western countries, the others being Russia, Japan and China.[10]

There are over 600,000 foreign students in Britain, the second most popular destination for international study after the US, which has well over a million foreign students.[11] Three-quarters of the international students in Britain are from outside Europe – China, India, Nigeria, and a host of other countries. They're usually paying £20,000 per year or more in tuition fees alone not to speak of what they pay for accommodation in university-owned hostels and what they spend in university cafeterias. This makes UK universities ever wealthier, ever more capable of financing world-class research and ever more attractive to scholarly talent from around the world. That virtuous circle again.

The fact that the academic race debate is centred in Western universities is itself a reflection of how dominant they are. South America is a more racially diverse space than the West, so one could well imagine South American universities being in the driving seat of the global race debate. Nor is there any good reason why universities in Africa, the continent arguably most affected by the racial hierarchy, should not be places where fresh perspectives on race originate and *are discussed elsewhere*. Yet nothing of the sort is happening.

Students and academics from around the world must go to US or UK universities if they want to be at the centre of the race debate, more so to have any impact on it. As a result, our *knowledge* of how race works is usually derived from the writings of one or other prominent US-based scholar whose perspectives on the issue are primarily shaped by the specific American context they inhabit. The debate on what is a global issue has thus become an incredibly Western-centric affair almost wholly focused on happenings in the US and to a lesser extent the UK, as if these were the only societies that matter in the discussion. A highly parochial perspective that is the outcome of the domination of Western academia in pretty much every 'global' intellectual discussion, including that on race.

A key source of this domination is the sphere of academic publishing, which is crucial for the spreading of scholarly knowledge across the globe. For a few years, I served on the editorial board of a niche British academic journal. It would be inappropriate of me to disclose figures but what I will say is that I was taken aback when I first learnt how much the working budget of this small journal amounted to. It was, in short, a fair figure, several times larger than most *major* African academic journals have at their disposal.

The money enabled the journal to finance workshops and research grants as well as dispatch editorial staff to international academic conferences. I knew from colleagues in African academic journals that it was extremely rare for them to be able to finance trips to academic conferences on other continents. Such underfinancing means they struggle to make their presence felt in global academia. They thus lack basic brand recognition, not to speak of prestige.

It is hence no coincidence that virtually all the world's top academic journals in terms of prestige and 'impact factor' – the frequency with which the average article in a journal is cited – are Western-based. Which means the most important academic journals in the world are run by predominantly white editorial boards. This positions black and brown academics at an immediate psychological and intellectual disadvantage.

If they seek *global* recognition as researchers, they need to be published in Western journals. This need often necessitates them reproducing Western thought paradigms in their article submissions. No one will ever demand they do this, but the reality of the matter is that if they want to be published in the *American* Journal of Political Science or the *British* Journal of

Politics and International Relations, they need to frame their articles in a manner they think will be persuasive to those who will decide whether it gets published or not. What do I mean by 'Western thought paradigms'?

For instance, Westerners and certainly Western academics generally believe liberal democracy is the ideal form of government everywhere. So, even if you don't agree with this assumption and want to argue on the way forward for this or that society, it is strategically useful for you to wrap your arguments around liberal democratic ideals if you want to be published in a respected Western journal. I know academics from various global South countries who *don't think* liberal democracy is the best way forward for their nations at this point in their history but pretend they do in their writings to indulge Western sensibilities and avoid marginalisation. This is how certain ways of thinking become privileged.

Another pressure non-Western scholars will feel is the need to situate their work on a side of whatever intellectual debate Western scholars are engrossed in at any given point in time. Otherwise, your work may not be deemed 'relevant'. Anyone who's been involved with Western academia knows the 'so what' question. Right from when you propose your PhD subject, you are required to provide a justification for why it should matter to anyone. Of course, you don't need to say much to justify why an analysis of a British or American phenomenon matters. But you will need to do a bit more to persuade Western scholars why an analysis of a Kenyan or Vietnamese phenomenon matters.

You will need to explain its *wider implications*, which is basically a demand that you make your discussion relevant to some bigger intra-Western discussion, such as that between liberals and conservatives, even though this debate interests precious few outside the West. For many Western academics, happenings in Africa and other non-Western regions are primarily useful as empirical examples, the academic equivalent of raw materials, to buttress this or that argument in their intra-Western intellectual disputes. Something to bash the other side on the head with: 'See? Africa's situation proves capitalism is the problem. No, it proves capitalism is the solution!' If you focus on an issue that won't serve any of the big Western intellectual camps in their battles, you'll likely have to deal with many disinterested looks.

Like in any other industry, most people go with the grain to get ahead, so non-Western scholars simply try to adapt to all this. Now, if there was a *Kenyan* Journal of Political Science or a *Pakistani* Journal of Politics and International Relations that were globally prestigious to publish in, the psychological playing field would be very different. Kenyan and Pakistani academics wouldn't need to pander to Western intellectual interests. There would be more options for non-Western scholars. Global academic status is determined by who has the power to make the ideas and issues they think matter *matter*. Western universities are undoubtedly the key centres of global knowledge production today.

One practical consequence of this is that whatever intellectual glory non-Western scholars achieve in Western academia ends up falling to them personally, of course, but in the bigger picture, also to the universities they work in and the nations those universities are located in. The AstraZeneca Covid-19 vaccine developed at Oxford University is seen as a *British* achievement. And while people in Britain see it as a multiracial country in which Britishness is not synonymous with whiteness, the average global citizen still associates Britain chiefly with its white majority. It should not be too difficult to see how all this has a bearing on sustaining white status.

As for the international students who attend Western universities, they don't just leave their money here, they are also exposed to Western ways of life and thinking which they carry back with them to their countries after finishing their studies. This is how the Harvards and Oxfords et al continue to shape the ideas of future elites around the world. The global status of Western universities enables Western governments to sow the seeds of their future influence today. And they go about this quite strategically indeed.

In 2014, the House of Lords published a report on *Persuasion and Power in the Modern World* which analysed the power resources and strategies Britain has at its disposal to exert its influence in the twenty-first century.[12] 'The UK has a number of national scholarships programmes *designed* to help build a strong international network of friends of the UK who *will rise to increasingly influential positions* over the years,' the report noted. A prominent example is the prestigious Chevening Scholarship programme, which is funded by the UK's Foreign, Commonwealth and Development Office, evidence it is an instrument of British *foreign policy*. The Chevening scholarships have resulted in an influential alumni network numbering over fifty thousand former students spread across the likes of China, Egypt, India, Indonesia, Malaysia, Mexico and South Korea, nations strategically selected for their emerging power status.

A survey of foreign alumni of another popular scheme, the Commonwealth Scholarships, found that 45 per cent of respondents had influenced their government's thinking in specific policy areas, and a quarter had held public office at some point in time.[13] As of 2021, a total of sixty-five serving world leaders – presidents and prime ministers – had studied at an American university while fifty-seven had attended one in Britain.[14] France was in third place, with thirty leaders having attended university in their country. All the top five countries in terms of number of world leaders having studied at their universities were white-majority nations.

Hugo Swire, a former Minister of State at the Foreign, Commonwealth and Development Office, emphasised how important it is for the British government to keep in touch with UK scholarship foreign alumni because they 'rise up in whatever sector of society – civil society, politics, sport or business – and you have them, so you need to keep them'.[15] Of course, one can't blame Britain for taking its influence-building seriously and developing strategies to further its interests. That is what nations who want to become or remain powerful do.

It would be no problem at all if *all* nations could build world-class universities, offer generous scholarship programmes, maintain contacts with their foreign alumni and exert greater or lesser global influence this way. The problem of course is that most nations don't have that level of available resources. And these tend to be black and brown nations.

Very little, if any, of all this is the result of conscious design on the part of (white) Western academics. Most would be appalled at the idea they are perpetuating any sort of racial order. Western academics are generally left leaning and often like to make a point of how critical they are of the West and its dominant status. There is a clear tendency for some to distinguish themselves from other whites as the whites who 'get it'.

But the reality is that you cannot be so overwhelmingly dominant in a global domain without most of the prestige and status in that domain accruing to you, irrespective of your intentions. And that positions you at the top of the pecking order. Today's situation is, to a large extent, the consequence of the incredible success of contemporary Western universities, especially those in the English-speaking world. It is not clear who exactly we can blame for them being so attractive to students and scholars from all over the world.

Despite coming under fire for being racist, Eurocentric and whatnot, they remain the universities better-off parents from the global South often send their children to be educated in. And the latter are not dragged there kicking and screaming either. They *want* to study at a British or American university because they believe they will get a better-quality education there than they would back home. And they are often right. Meanwhile, even the wokest Western youths don't seem eager to go to study in universities outside the West, which says something as well.

Ultimately, the resources Western universities have at their disposal mean that aside from them monopolising global prestige in the sphere of knowledge production, they inadvertently limit the growing potential of universities elsewhere who keep losing scholarly talent to them, ultimately perpetuating the existing order. If countries elsewhere are not able to build universities that can effectively compete with those in the West, then Western academia will continue to dominate global knowledge production with all the practical consequences.

And those consequences are no small matter, for aside from the power of knowledge in and of itself, domination in the sphere of higher education is closely linked to domination in another key sphere of our lives today: technology. The role of technology is hardly ever discussed in the race debate. Let us now move to that subject, for it has been playing a key role in shaping the global order for a while now and importantly, will do so even more in this century.

6

Technology and race

Growing up in Nigeria, we used to hear stories about how Europeans had bedazzled our ancestors by holding out mirrors in front of them. Because it was a novel object to many Africans all those centuries ago, its reflective effects appeared magical to them, and the white man a special being for possessing such wizardry. These anecdotal tales were usually narrated in the spirit of highlighting how mercilessly the white man had exploited his technological advantage over us in the past, the moral being that we must never let it happen again.

It is difficult to dispute Nigerian historian Toyin Falola's observation that 'the success of the European conquest was largely dependent on technological superiority, one that exposed the underdeveloped science and technology in Africa'.[1] The same point applies to many other parts of the world successfully colonised by white people in centuries past. From the Europeans who seized the lands of the Native Americans to those who ended up ruling most of Africa and Asia, technology, especially the military kind, played a key role in their ability to dominate.

Yet the influence of technology in sustaining today's order, and white status specifically, is underemphasised in the race debate. Very wrongly so, for as Falola has also pointed out, 'from the ordinary mirror to the complex truck, products of technology are not just statements about consumption but also about the reality of power'. Technology reveals not just where power lies today but where it will likely lie tomorrow.

'Over the coming decade, the ability to advance and exploit science and technology will be an increasingly important metric of global power, conferring economic, political and military advantages . . . countries which establish a leading role in critical and emerging technologies will be at the forefront of global leadership,' noted the UK government's 2021 Integrated Review of Security, Defence, Development and Foreign Policy, a national strategy document.[2]

While associated with complexity, technology boils down to the creation of a material means to a material end. Up until the fifteenth century, Europeans chiefly borrowed technologies developed in Asia and elsewhere. At the beginning of the fifteenth century, Chinese ships were considered far superior to their European equivalents; they were larger, sturdier, more comfortable, and generally better suited for the crucial task of navigating long distances. However, China thereafter turned inwards and lost its technological mojo.

By the late seventeenth century, Europe had the best ships and deadliest weapons. The real technological game-changer, though, was Britain's Industrial Revolution which, from the mid-eighteenth century onwards, enabled it to manufacture goods on an unprecedented scale. Some today emphasise that Britain was able to finance these innovations only thanks to profits from being the main slave-trading nation of the seventeenth and eighteenth centuries. British historians prefer to point to the relatively open society, for that era, which encouraged individual initiative and fostered social mobility. What matters for consequence is that Britain and Western Europe as a whole emerged as the world's leading technology hub during this period.

In what would be a sign of things to come, eighteenth-century British governments actively supported what we today call Research and Development (R&D). In 1714, the British parliament passed the Longitude Act, offering an astronomical (at the time) £20,000 reward for the development of a marine chronometer capable of establishing longitude at sea. Most of the prize money went to John Harrison for his chronometer invention.[3] Armed with a replica of Harrison's gadget, Captain James Cook was able to explore and map the 'new world' territories now known as Australia and New Zealand. The rest is history.

Britain's technological innovations helped provide it with the financial and military muscle needed to establish an empire which by 1913 ruled over 412 million people, a quarter of the world's population. The economic effect of this period is visible in the fact that between 1820 and 1913, British per capita income grew faster than at any time in its previous history — three times as fast as in 1700-1820.[4] By 1913, it had reached roughly $5000 before the First World War disrupted things. Crucially from a wider racial perspective, this massive wealth growth was not restricted to Britain alone. Western Europe saw its GDP per capita triple during this period to a regional average of $3700. The white settler colonies of Australia, the US, Canada and New

Zealand saw even greater wealth growth. US per capita income quadrupled during this period while Canada's grew fivefold. In the cases of Australia and New Zealand, their per capita incomes multiplied twelvefold, with all four countries converging around the $5000 mark by 1913. Latin America, where many Europeans had settled, also saw its incomes double.

In contrast, colonised Asia's GDP per capita barely budged between 1820 and 1913, going from $579 to $679. Same for colonial Africa, where the figures stood at $418 and $585 respectively. The situation in the likewise mostly colonised Middle East was no different. That period, between 1820 and 1913, was when the white West truly established its wealth advantage over the rest of the world. Without technology, none of this would have been physically or psychologically possible. Europe's technological achievements fostered a self-belief in its civilisational-cum-racial superiority. In the idea whites were simply smarter than others. At the same time, it inspired the awe and sometimes fear of colonised black and brown peoples.

So, what say the technology status quo today? The Global Innovation Index measures national capacities in IT infrastructure, research capacity, knowledge production, human capital, market sophistication and institutions. Of the twenty highest-ranked countries in its 2022 survey, fourteen were Western nations.[5] Bar Israel, all the other members of the top twenty were in East Asia – South Korea, Singapore, China, Hong Kong (ranked separately from China) and Japan. The highest-ranked black-majority nation was South Africa, which came in at sixty-first position.

Having overtaken Europe technologically in the twentieth century, North America is now the most innovative continent in the world, followed by Europe, with Asia fast closing the gap while others struggle to keep up. In 2022, the ten biggest tech firms in the world in terms of sales and market value were Apple, Alphabet (parent company of Google), Microsoft, Samsung, Tencent, Meta (Facebook rebranded), Intel, Taiwan Semi-Conductor Manufacturing, Cisco and IBM. All ten are either based in the US or East Asia.[6]

Thanks to the humongous amount of personal data these firms gather, they have increasing power over how people spend their time, what professional opportunities they pursue, what social issues they discuss and how they view the world in general. Those who own these tech beasts and by extension the hundreds of smaller tech companies they own outright or control, will have some of the greatest influence in shaping the future global order. Suffice to say there is no black-owned tech giant today but plenty of white-owned ones.

In national terms, China is very close to neutralising the technological advantage it lost to the West several centuries ago. Currently ranked the eleventh most innovative nation in the world, it is now the world's top filer of international patents. Aside from China and long-time tech gurus like Japan and South Korea, other non-white nations making great technological strides include Turkey, Vietnam and, of course, India. These are the potential technological powerhouses of the future.

It is not that there is no innovation going on elsewhere, there is lots. According to the Global Innovation Index report, Sub-Saharan Africa has the largest number of economies 'overperforming' on the technological front. What is meant by this is that African countries are doing much better than might be expected *considering their limited resources.* There has been a massive growth in tech hubs across the continent, numbering 618 as at 2019.[7] Africa's key tech centres are in Nigeria, Kenya, Egypt and South Africa. These hubs form the backbone of its technological ecosystem and people there are coming up with plenty of fantastic ideas and products. But they are, as usual, chiefly constrained by a lack of adequate funding.

It is extremely difficult for poor countries to compete with rich countries in technology. Africa as a whole accounts for just *1 per cent* of global investment in Research and Development.[8] Meanwhile, rich countries usually invest 2–3 per cent of their *large* GDPs on R&D. The UK government has committed to spending 2.4 per cent of Britain's GDP on research and development by 2027, a figure amounting to tens of billions of dollars. Not to mention what the private sector is spending. A major reason China has made such huge strides towards closing the technological gap with the West is because it has been spending bucketloads of money on the effort every year – $441 billion in 2021 alone.[9] Only America spends more. Meanwhile, South Korea's $75 billion R&D expenditure is twice Nigeria's entire national budget.[10]

As Jeffrey Sachs explained in his book *The End of Poverty*, capital is always willing to pour money into technological projects in rich nations because it figures the rewards are inevitably huge. The buying power of rich country nationals incentivises it to create innovative products in those countries for the simple reason that it is sure people there can afford them. As a result, productivity usually improves steadily in the wealthiest markets, expanding them and creating more incentives for even more innovation. That damn virtuous circle again.

In poorer, less stable economies, especially those with smaller populations, even entrepreneurs with some capital are reluctant to risk investing much in innovation as they can't be sure they'll recoup their investments. Coming up with an innovative product in Zambia offers different rewards from coming up with one in Britain, not to speak of America. As a result, most times, innovation processes never get off the ground in poor countries. Even when their nationals have great ideas, these remain trapped in their heads. Or those nationals end up migrating to a rich country. The Zambian takes their ideas to Britain, America, or Canada where they can be brought to life. And while that Zambian will certainly benefit from such a move personally, Zambia won't.

A 2021 open letter by African scientists to the continent's governments emphasised how the lack of funding for R&D had made Africa dependent on the West for Covid vaccines during the pandemic.[11] Moreover, its over-reliance on international funding was contributing to the under-representation of black people in decisional R&D spaces, the scientists pointed out. African leaders will likely point to their budgets and argue they struggle to provide basic services. Where on earth are they supposed to find billions to spend on developing new technologies?

Some of the richer African nations could certainly afford to do more even with the limited resources they do have. Nigeria spends just 0.5 per cent of its GDP on Research and Development, compared to the global 2.2 per cent average. So, there is the question of some ruling elites simply not getting their priorities right. But most poor nations genuinely can't afford to support even basic research with well-equipped labs and universities, much less create the enabling environment needed for the ecosystem of scientists, researchers and institutions you need in order to go from an innovative idea to a finished product.

Even modern-day technologies considered obvious in rich countries are not always accessible in poor ones. As of 2021, more than a third of the world's population had *never* been online; 96 per cent of them live in developing countries.[12] In rich United Arab Emirates, 99 per cent of the population have internet access;[13] in South Sudan, 89 per cent don't.[14] The result of all this is that most innovative activities simply make the usually white rich world richer, exacerbating racial inequalities and hierarchies even further.

To get an insider's view on the African world of technology and start-ups, I spoke to Iyinoluwa Aboyeji, a highly successful thirty-one-year-old Nigerian entrepreneur who has co-founded two 'unicorns'. A unicorn is a private start-up valued at over $1 billion. I asked what his experience had been like persuading investors to back his projects when they were just ideas. 'In my first start-up which I established when I lived in Canada, I positioned myself as a leader and emphasised my focus was on Africa. That was a double whammy against me in the eyes of investors. The face of the company was African, and the company was focused on Africa which they considered too poor to be worth investing in,' Aboyeji recalled. He quickly discovered he wasn't getting nearly as many investor meetings as his Western peers.

By the time he started his subsequent company, Andela, a job placement network for software developers, he 'understood the game'. He picked as the face of his company a white co-founder Western investors knew. 'Everything was so much easier,' Aboyeji recalled. 'I had to be validated by a white partner who assured others there was some money to be made in Africa, otherwise I would not have been able to raise the capital I did for Andela,' he said. The company then went on to become a unicorn.

When he started his next major project, Flutterwave, a financial technology firm, Aboyeji tried a different strategy. This time he was bent on proving black people could 'do it on their own' so he founded the company with solely Nigerian partners. However, despite the huge success of his previous start-up, he again struggled to raise international finance. In the end, he and his partners were fortunate to get some early investments from Nigerians and South Africans. 'Black capital had to come to the rescue,' he recalled.

Aboyeji emphasised that he and his Nigerian partners were lucky because there is some local capital in Nigeria and South Africa. It's much tougher for entrepreneurs in other usually poorer African nations where capital is extremely scarce. Aboyeji said one thing he has learned from his experience is that 'money is not neutral; it has a point of view'. The way he sees it, the appropriate response to racism in the capital space is 'not an appeal to equality but building your own capital stock and being very intentional about where it goes'. In other words, putting your money in black hands as often as you can.

His story reveals both the opportunities for Africans in the ever-expanding tech space and the challenges they face as a result of the capital shortage the continent suffers from and general disregard. Within tech spaces in capital-rich America, blackness can elicit similar dismissive attitudes.

The Princeton academic Ruha Benjamin's book *Race after Technology* provides a rare glimpse into the nexus between the two in the US.[15]

It cites the story of a former (likely white) Apple employee who described his experience on a team that was developing speech recognition for Siri, the virtual assistant program. As they worked on different English dialects – Australian, Singaporean and Indian English – the employee asked his boss: 'What about African American English?' To which his boss responded: 'Well, Apple products are for the premium market.'

This happened just a year after Apple had bought Beats, a company co-founded by Dr Dre, for $3 billion, highlighting again how individual black success stories do not have the power to alter the general associations of blackness with poverty relative to other groups in America. One black computer scientist complained of how market pressures affected his own decisions too, saying 'it would be interesting to have a black guy talk as the voice [for his app] but we don't want to create friction either. First, we need to sell products.' This led Benjamin to observe that 'even a Black computer scientist running his own company who earnestly wants to encode a different voice into his app is still hemmed in by the desire of many people for white-sounding voices'.

Where does this desire come from today? Racism is too general an answer, especially when it comes to people not white sharing such a desire. Part of it can be that people have simply become used to hearing 'white-sounding voices' in apps which are often produced with affluent white consumers in mind. We often defer to the familiar, including when it comes to accents. But there's more to it than that. Accents are also associated with status. Every society has its own hierarchy of accents. Regional German accents are seen as less desirable than standard German in Germany while in Switzerland people prefer their surgeon to have a Swiss German accent than a standard German one.[16]

In the English-speaking world, Americans favour British accents over Indian accents and perceive those who speak with Mexican or Greek accents as less intelligent and professional than those who speak 'standard' US English. In Britain, people regularly distinguish between those who 'sound posh' and those who don't. While British racial attitudes have changed over the past half-century, attitudes towards accents have remained remarkably stable. A 2019 study showed that just like in 1969, accents associated with 'Queen's English' and 'Edinburgh English' were considered prestigious while Birmingham accents, many southern working-class accents and Afro-Caribbean accents were considered the least prestigious.[17]

Nigerian teachers who have lived in Britain or America and thus speak English with a British or American accent are highly valued in private Nigerian primary and secondary schools because parents will pay a premium for their children to be taught by teachers who speak with these accents. Nigerian elites prefer their children to sound British or American as they (rightly) assume this will give them an advantage in international settings in a way sounding Nigerian will not.

I seriously doubt an Alexa that spoke English sounding like a Nigerian would be popular with Indian consumers and vice versa. Most Indian and Nigerian consumers would prefer the version that speaks with a generic (white) British or American accent. Not just because they are used to them but because they associate them with status and people want as much status as possible present in their lives. Even if it's just in the form of a white-sounding Alexa in their living room. I strongly suspect if black people were the wealthiest highest-status racial group, attitudes to 'black-sounding' voices would be quite different.

But there are many significantly more serious issues regarding race and technology such as algorithms that discriminate against people of colour. One study of over a hundred facial-recognition algorithms found that they falsely identified African American and Asian faces ten to one hundred times more than white faces.[18] Facial recognition is a major technology used in policing and general surveillance these days. The issue of facial analysis algorithms misidentifying black people was explored in the Netflix documentary *Coded Bias*. In the US, there have also been reports of mortgage algorithms used by online lenders to determine rates for loan applicants using flawed data to assess black and Latino borrowers, costing them up to half a billion dollars more in interest every year than their white counterparts.[19] 'Techno-racism' is the term that has been coined for instances of the misperceptions or bias of tech designers creeping into their algorithm models and having real-world effects.

It's unlikely we'd be talking about any of this if Silicon Valley had sprung up in Nigeria or India rather than north California, or if black and brown people owned the Apples, Microsofts and Googles of this world and were the affluent consumers designers kept in mind to ensure they sold products. As it is, the only viable response to techno-racism today is to keep a close eye on the kind of data being deployed to build profiles in various devices, what has been dubbed 'algorithmic accountability'.

There is clearly more racial diversity in Silicon Valley today than there used to be, especially when it comes to Asian Americans. Alphabet, Microsoft and Zoom have Asian American CEOs. At Meta, employees of Asian descent now outnumber white employees.[20] Those who run Silicon Valley like to portray it as a completely meritocratic post-racial environment. However, even among its generally successful Asian American workforce, there are still complaints of it being more difficult for them to break into leadership ranks than whites, of fundraising being way more difficult if you have any form of an Asian accent, of dealing with the 'forever foreigner' stereotype implying they have split loyalties to the US and their ancestral home, or of having to put up with various casual stereotypical remarks about their Asianness.

And when it comes to other non-white groups, big tech employs few black or Hispanic workers and hardly any in technical or executive roles.[21] Even if things were to change for the better with regards to the treatment of racial minorities in Silicon Valley, we'd still be left with a tech world in which, similar to academia, power and status largely reside in the West.

And just like in academia, one of the major reasons for this is that wealthy nations are consistently able to draw talent from elsewhere to improve their tech ecosystems. Britain's government has now established an Office for Talent to make it 'easier for those with the most talent, potential, energy and creativity to come to the UK from around the world – reaching out to those with the skills the UK needs and helping them to understand the opportunities on offer'. It is supported by the new points-based immigration system designed to favour such individuals and is already seeing results with a wave of Nigerian techies relocating to the UK in the past two years.

Technology is not just a benign force changing our everyday lives, it is an arena of increasingly fierce competition between nations. Those who gain a strategic advantage in emerging technologies like engineering biology, quantum computing and Artificial Intelligence will be at the top of the global pecking order this century. The increased efficiencies brought about by these technologies will see power and wealth accrue mostly to those states at the forefront of those technologies. AI alone is projected to add $16 trillion to the global economy by 2030,[22] while 5G is projected to generate $13 trillion in added economic value by 2035.[23] For now, most of the candidates for these leading roles are white-majority nations and Asian nations, all pouring huge sums into these spheres.

This will provide many personal opportunities to clever minds with great ideas from around the world and one can hardly blame Britain or any other rich nation for wanting to attract such people, much less those who decide to take up their offers. But the practical consequence of this tech brain drain is that it ultimately condemns certain parts of the world, usually its black and brown parts, to remain primarily consumers, not producers, of technology.

And when it comes to global status hierarchies, *consumers* of technology are not conferred the same prestige as *producers* of technology. Even the former sometimes don't see themselves as the equals of the latter because they are wowed by their gadgets. Much of the mystique around whiteness in recent centuries revolves around its associations with technology. Today, it's not mirrors but space rockets that are often described as evidence of 'the white man's magic' in Africa. The material capacity to produce that wow reaction in others still often rests in white hands, perpetuating white status and prestige.

7

Western media,
the news arm of whiteness?

'It is not just ogres like Trump who spread the gospel of white supremacy. Much of the liberal Western press is deeply invested in the project through its characterisation of news events depending on where in the world they happen and who they happen to,' wrote Patrick Gathara, a popular Kenyan journalist, in a 2021 article for Al Jazeera's website.[1] This is a claim more than a few outside the West would agree with. There was much anger in many parts of the world at the way Western media covered the most significant news story of 2022 – Russia's invasion of Ukraine – an event which in and of itself had nothing to do with race.

In an article for CNN, Moky Makura, a Nigerian writer and media observer, argued that Western media outlets from America's CBS to Britain's ITV were reporting the event 'in ways that illustrate deep bias, informed by a belief system that screams of an old-world, White-led order'.[2] As an example, she cited ITV correspondent Lucy Watson's reporting on the invasion of Ukraine: 'The unthinkable has happened . . . this is not a developing, third-world nation; this is Europe!' Meanwhile, reporting from Kyiv, CBS correspondent Charlie D'Agata commented that Ukraine was not a place 'like Iraq or Afghanistan, that has seen conflict raging for decades . . . You know, this is a *relatively civilised, relatively European* city where you wouldn't expect that.'[3]

Nota bene, D'Agata's description of Ukraine as 'relatively' civilised and European was a great example of hierarchy constructions within whiteness from the perspective of a white Westerner (D'Agata is an American). Ukrainians could well have been offended to have been described as only 'relatively' civilised and European! However, the CBS correspondent's comments understandably sparked the outrage of many chiefly for their implicit depiction of the Middle East as a violent uncivilised place. There were also angry reactions to a *Daily Telegraph* article which started out by asserting, 'They [Ukrainians] seem so like us. That is what makes it so shocking. War is no longer something visited upon impoverished and remote populations. It can happen to anyone.'[4]

These kinds of comments in top tier Western media provoked a letter of protest from Africa's Foreign Press Association.[5] 'Various iterations on the theme that it is unthinkable to see violence in countries populated by white people, reinforce views that already exist systematically in societies at large,' the letter stated. It pointed out that 'People who are not white are not more innately prone and habituated to violence and suffering . . . this attitude has been a feature of Western media coverage for decades. It is glaring in the lack of dignity afforded to black and brown-skinned victims of conflict.'

Several years ago, provoked by an experience I had while being interviewed on TV, I wrote an article in the *Guardian* titled 'Why Africans worry about how Africa is portrayed in Western media', where I tried to explain why all this matters to so many people. It's no secret Africans have long complained about Western media regularly portraying their continent as backwards and chaotically violent. Just as people from the Middle East have long bemoaned the focus on terrorism and strife in their region. What is symptomatic is that in my case, and I suspect in Gathara and Makura's as well, *where* we chose to write about Western media was not accidental and reveals the power dynamic at the heart of the problem today.

I could have chosen to write my article on Western media in a Nigerian newspaper or media website, as could fellow Nigerian Makura. Gathara could have written his for a Kenyan media outlet. But would our complaints have gotten any *international* notice if we'd done so? Doubtful. Because how many non-Africans consume African media? There are, in fact, only a handful of media in the world that can claim to be truly *global* media.

To be global means you have significant demographically diverse audiences on all continents, enjoy brand recognition around the world and have the capacity to cover international events as they unfold in real time. Al Jazeera aside, virtually all the media that have these attributes today are Western based. Hence, the ironic situation in which complaints about Western media coverage are most effective when made in Western media! Even when we want to complain about them, we have to do it *through* them. Because they are the ones the world watches and listens to.

Growing up in Nigeria, we got our news about the world from CNN and the BBC. At first glance, the media landscape today is radically different from what it was then. News distribution is way more decentralised today, some might even say deterritorialised. An individual in Nigeria, Brazil or Pakistan can post a news item on Twitter that catches fire globally and before you know it, people from all over the world are commenting on it and disseminating it further.

When social-media-savvy Nigerian youths initiated the *#EndSARS* protests against Nigerian police brutality in 2020, my students here in Britain knew what was going on, sometimes in surprising (to me) detail. They knew what was going on from Twitter, not from the BBC. That social media has changed the news business is indisputable. Nevertheless, attention-grabbing events like the #EndSARS protests are not regular occurrences but things that happen once in a while. Sporadic social-media-driven stories aside, the *systematic* production of news that is viewed *around the world* is still very much a Western-dominated affair. And despite many critical opinions about them in the global South, Western media are still the go-to media for international news for people in that part of the world as well.

In 2021, the BBC achieved record international audience figures with an average audience of 489 million adults every week, an increase of over twenty million from the previous year.[6] It was on course to hit five hundred million by 2022. Sixty million Indians, thirty-seven million Nigerians, fifteen million Kenyans, thirteen million Iranians and eight million Pakistanis regularly consume BBC content, among others around the world. No non-Western media comes close to having such a sizeable intercontinental audience. As one Bloomberg columnist put it, the BBC 'spans the world as effortlessly as the Royal Navy once did'.[7] Indeed.

The British broadcaster and other western outlets dominate not just the airwaves but the digital news-sphere as well. As at September 2022, the BBC was the world's number one news website in terms of traffic. MSN, Microsoft's news aggregation portal, was in second place, followed by CNN. All the ten most-visited global news sites were Western-based and owned.[8] Aside from sheer traffic volume on their sites, the most famous Western media brands also enjoy more global credibility and prestige than their competitors elsewhere.

As someone who has written for a variety of media, I know having your article published by, say, the *Financial Times*, still impresses most people today, including, perhaps even especially, people in the global South. If the *New York Times* publishes your piece, you're seen as a world-class writer. And if you do something for *New Yorker* magazine, you're basically writing royalty. People around the world care what *The Economist* publishes about the situation in their countries. They may resent its takes and spend half the day criticising what it has written about their country on Twitter, but that is because they know people around the world pay attention to its articles. No media in Asia, Africa, South America or anywhere else have such global standing.

News has always travelled across borders as people have been sharing stories, rumours and gossip about events and people in other places for as long as they have moved around. But it was not until the nineteenth century that news production became an organised affair. The pioneer global media actor was Agence France-Presse (AFP), the world's first news agency, founded in Paris in 1835. Not long after, in 1846, the Associated Press (AP) was established in the United States while Reuters was created in 1851 in London. These agencies became the first producers of the commodity called 'news'. The BBC was founded a century ago, in 1922. It was joined in that decade by the likes of CBS and NBC, while CNN and Sky News were established much later, in 1980 and 1989 respectively. These media would come to dominate the global news landscape in the twentieth century.

The cultural capital Western media have acquired over the years, along with their financial muscle and often very high-quality journalism, has not disappeared into a digital ether. Western media are the most criticised media precisely because people know they are the *most influential* media. Otherwise, no one would care what they say. So, a key question for us here: Is Western media 'deeply invested' in white supremacy as the quote at the beginning of the chapter suggested?

While I've written for various Western media outlets over the years, it was in Poland that I worked as an actual full-time journalist. Polish media is not considered Western media, so to get an insider's take, I spoke to a black journalist who's been in the industry for decades and is today highly positioned in one of the major Western players. Let's call this person X. Before we proceed, it's worth noting there are some basic rules journalists everywhere follow when deciding what is a *newsworthy* story and what isn't. They are encapsulated in industry wisdoms like 'If it bleeds it leads' and 'Dog bites man not interesting, man bites dog interesting.'

People are drawn to violence and the unexpected. So news media often focus on stories that feed this interest. The differences between media around the world are less in what kind of stories they cover than in *how* those stories are covered. In X's experience, Western news editors have usually chosen the path of least resistance when deciding on the hows of coverage. A path that leans heavily into the conventional wisdoms, stereotypes if you prefer, shared by their audiences.

From the editor's perspective, this is easier than covering things from perspectives their audiences are not familiar with or in terms that don't trigger instant associations in their minds. 'People have always used shorthand to understand the world,' X stated. 'Hence, I had to fight long battles for us to stop discussing "Africa" like it were a single country or describing a popular African TV personality as the Kenyan or Nigerian Oprah.' Coverage details were decided by usually white editors who went with what they and their audiences were used to. These decision-makers themselves usually had scant everyday contact with people of colour. In line with the *poor them* attitudes of the white progressives who dominate Western media teams, they tended, for instance, to view black people as 'passive actors in need of saving' which informed their coverage of Africa as a place of suffering and helplessness.

But lack of knowledge was not the only problem. Although wisdoms like 'if it bleeds it leads' are supposed to be iron rules, in practice they tend to be relative. A lot depends on *who* bleeds. Historically, black and brown victims of crimes have not been considered as newsworthy as white victims, X said, recalling once being sent to cover the murder of a fifteen-year-old girl that was so uniquely gruesome, editors had it penned down as a sure story for the day.

X was able to interview the parents of the murdered girl, get pictures of her, everything deemed necessary for a 'good story'. Yet, when the news editors learnt the murdered girl was mixed-race, not white as they had initially thought, they lost interest in the story and it was canned. 'In isolation, you might class such incidents as simple editorial calls. But put together, they manifested a clear lack of equality between white audiences and others,' X commented.

Today, there are more people of colour in decision-making positions in Western media and such double standards are being questioned from within these organisations. In addition to this, social media has transformed the environment they operate in. 'Previously, people of colour could curse into their TV screens when they heard or saw something they didn't like and that was it. Western media could say what they wanted without having to worry how it was being received,' X observed. Today, they get instant feedback from the public.

Twitter et al have enabled black and brown audiences to talk back at Western media. They now know they can be called out, so they're more careful how they go about things – the last thing any media wants is audience backlash. X went as far as to say social media has 'enabled a new wave of anti-colonialism', insisting, however, that 'there is no agenda' to portray people of colour in a negative light and propagate white supremacy. 'I know many black and brown people think this, but it's a myth. What *is* true is that despite my position today, I still need a higher-up usually white gatekeeper to OK what I'm doing in general. This is where we get to the critical issue of *ownership*,' X observed.

The journalist cited Tyler Perry, the black American entertainment mogul, as an example of how the dynamic can work differently. Thanks to having his own production company, 'he tells our stories the way he wants to tell them. He chooses the script, the cast, everything. That is the power of ownership. We have to create our own media companies to tell our stories because the Western ones are not serving us well enough. There continues to be a higher bar for news from Africa and Asia to make it onto the global news agenda.'

The big obstacle to this is, of course, financial. Establishing a media organisation capable of competing with the Western behemoths for global influence would require billions. The BBC enjoyed a revenue of £5.3 billion for the 2021/2022 period.[9] South African Broadcasting Corporation (SABC), probably the wealthiest media house in Africa, had a revenue 5 per cent that amount.[10] There is no way it could effectively compete with a BBC or CNN for global attention.

There are of course new forms of digital media that don't require billions in investment and can be quite effective. Even the media behemoths of today can no longer rely on just TV or newspaper content for influence, they increasingly combine a mix of material from these traditional sources with social media content to stay relevant. Nevertheless, if we're talking about achieving truly opinion-shaping influence, you'd still need a significant investment to get such an outfit going, to keep it going before it starts making enough money to run itself, and to market it.

As I mentioned earlier, the Qatari-government-owned Al Jazeera is the only non-Western media with truly global reach thanks to the fact it is well funded and can employ world-class journalists as well as build state-of-the-art studios. What about the English-language China Global Television Network (CGTV), owned by state media behemoth, China Central Television (CCTV)? If it's an issue of money, surely, they have a lot of it, some could point out. Why haven't *they* been able to shake the dominant status of Western media?

The Chinese have indeed spent a ton of money in recent years trying to change the global media landscape to boost their country's soft power. They have invested in top-notch studios for CGTV. China woos journalists from around the world with all-expenses-paid tours of their country and offers scholarships to study journalism at Chinese universities. The objective of all this, in the words of Chinese President Xi Jinping, is to 'tell China's story well'.

Yet, despite money not being a problem in this case, Chinese efforts at upending western media domination via CGTV have been hampered by the *too obviously* propagandistic role of their station. People recognise it is an arm of China's government. And people don't like the idea of being influenced by the governments of other countries. They are more relaxed about being influenced by the corporations of other countries, which goes to show how successful both nationalism and capitalism have been. The idea of a foreign government trying to shape our thinking grates on our nationalist sentiments, the idea of a foreign corporation doing the same we have accepted as par for the course. Western media are not seen as direct arms of their governments but as more or less 'independent' media.

And indeed, people all over the world watched CNN and other American media go after Donald Trump throughout his presidency. They hear British prime ministers and governments constantly criticised on Sky News and the BBC, even though the latter is a public media. You're unlikely to hear many critical comments about Xi Jinping and the Chinese government on CGTV. Despite exploding on the global scene in its initial years, even Al Jazeera is increasingly viewed today as a too obvious propaganda tool of the Qatari royal family, though it still has way more credibility than CGTV.

Some may scoff that this is all an illusion, that Western media are as much propaganda tools as media from elsewhere. But the billions who watch and listen to them around the world clearly find them at least somewhat credible. And that is what matters for global news-shaping power. Like Western universities, Western media lead the way in their industry.

The biggest media houses enjoy close to monopoly status. Those that are privately owned are usually in the hands of white magnates like Rupert Murdoch, who owns everything from newspapers to TV stations. It is thus pretty much white people running the global media show. Black and brown journalists can, at best, work *for* them. That is not a level racial field by any stretch of the imagination.

There is a link between this status quo and the way news like the invasion of a white nation is covered. One of the most powerful and honest scenes I've watched on television was in a movie about Western journalists in Rwanda during the genocide, I unfortunately can't remember the title. In the scene, a white female journalist was telling her white male colleague about her feelings covering the genocide in Rwanda compared to those covering the war in Yugoslavia a few years earlier. She said something like this: 'Each time I saw a child lying dead on the streets of Sarajevo, I felt anguish. Actual physical pain . . . But here I see the same thing happening to children and . . . I feel . . . nothing.'

Aside from the empathy asymmetry in *global media*, another consequence of the status quo is that non-Western countries usually get mentioned only if a crisis or bizarre event occurs on their territory. Non-shocking non-unique events are only deemed newsworthy if they happen in powerful countries. Elections in Britain are deemed newsworthy in a way elections in Bangladesh are not, despite nearly three times as many people inhabiting the latter as the former. This asymmetry infuses media in the global South as well. Nigerian media often report news from America, but American media rarely report news from Nigeria. When it comes to world news, lower-status nations pay attention to high-status nations, but the latter do not reciprocate.

All this means that the average statistically white Western citizen is likely to learn not much about the black and brown nations of this world while the citizens of the global South often learn more about the West than their own regions! The power asymmetry leads to a knowledge asymmetry, one where black and brown people know arguably *too much* about the Western world and too little about their own. Which of course only enhances Western-nation brand familiarity and soft power.

The fact the world still cares a lot what Western media says reflects not just the power of those media or even their mother nations, but of whiteness as a whole. After all, the white Brit, American or German doesn't give two hoots how their nation is portrayed in Nigerian, Indian or Brazilian media. They don't care because they don't have to. They are confident, often to the point of arrogance, in the strength of their national brands and can't imagine the image of Britishness, Americanness or Germanness being damageable by the media of the global South.

Moreover, as mentioned in the chapter on borders, white Westerners today are not migrating to the global South in large numbers or working for people from that part of the world. Their futures are thus not dependent on what Africans, Asians, South Americans or Arabs think of them. In contrast, us non-whites living in the West fret about perceptions of our home nations as our futures often depend on the opinions of the white majorities in the societies we inhabit.

People of African descent are often frustrated with the way Africa is presented in Western media because we know it affects how non-Africans view us and our capabilities. As discussed earlier, just as Western economic success has helped create a positive stereotype of whiteness, so a perceived African lack of it has helped perpetuate negative stereotypes of blackness. Black professionals in the UK, especially those who grew up in Africa and thus operate without the cover of a British accent, often complain of being underestimated in their workplaces. It is assumed that since they attended schools in a poor backward environment (as many presume all Africa is), they can't possibly be that terribly knowledgeable, now can they? For this group, every news story presenting Africa in a negative light is seen as something that will only make their everyday working lives that much harder. This can often produce defensive reactions.

Naturally, black people want to be treated as equals by those they encounter in international settings. No one likes being patronised. So, the middle-class professional black folk that tend to be the ones who find themselves in international settings are often frustrated with Western media images of starving children and other pictures of poverty in Africa. Because they know this helps shape how they themselves will be perceived here – as people associated with poverty and failure. It is this association with failure that individually successful blacks especially find particularly infuriating.

Perhaps even worse is the awareness in the black diaspora that the regular media portrayals of dysfunctionality in Africa, however well intentioned, help nurture the colonialist narrative of black people being incapable of efficient self-government. For successful blacks who feel individually no less capable than their white counterparts, these images of Africa continue to cast an uncomplimentary shadow that can appear frustratingly near impossible to shake off.

In an era preoccupied with 'narrative', some of the diaspora here can thus sometimes end up more concerned with media perceptions of Africa than with the realities of Africa. The actual suffering can elicit less outrage than the fact it is being exposed for others to see. But the reality is what it is. I once had a revealing conversation with someone who worked in a British aid agency trying to recalibrate its messaging and advertisements to be more racially sensitive.

The agency was surprised by the fact that when they showed samples of new fundraising charity ads to a community in Africa that was the subject of those ads, the community's leaders expressed concern that their situation was not depicted *drastically enough*. They wanted the world to know things were really difficult for them and that they desperately needed help. They were focused on the realities of their everyday lives and not on how images from Africa affected its status in the eyes of the world. The latter is a concern of the continent's more privileged classes. In our discussions around Western media portrayals of Africa, those of us in more comfortable situations should not forget that there is thus as much to be done in the sphere of Africa's reality as in the realm of outside perceptions of it.

The main problem when it comes to the perception question is that Africans, and black people in general, have no global microphone of their own with which to tell their news stories the way they want them told. They usually have to rely on the magnanimity of Western media. And while many Western media organisations are increasingly keen to showcase racially diverse voices in order to make themselves more attractive for global audiences, they remain under predominantly (white) Western control. This gives white folk the main say over the global news agenda and the ability to enhance the image of their nations, which only leads to more wealth, status and global power for them and the West in general. It is difficult to imagine how that could change if others don't find some way to build their own BBCs.

8

International influence

International institutions are another major source of status and power in the global environment today. A 2014 House of Lords report titled 'Persuasion and Power in the Modern World' described Britain as 'one of the most networked countries in the world with an important institutional position in the . . . G20, G8, NATO, UN Security Council, IMF, World Bank and Commonwealth.'[1] British influence in these key institutions which *'helped promote its interests over the past sixty years*, is a central pillar of its soft power', the report suggested.

A defining feature of the international organisations that maintain today's order is that a significant number of white-majority nations can lay claim to 'important institutional positions' within them in a way few non-white nations can. I'm not just talking about the usual suspects, the likes of Britain, France, Russia, Germany or the US. These are all large or very objectively powerful nations, and the fact powerful states use global institutions to maintain and increase their influence will hardly surprise most readers. What is more revealing is that there are nations who are *minor* actors within the white world, yet very influential on the world stage, often more so than nations of the global South several times their size and population.

Take the situation in the United Nations, the world's central global institution today. Historically, national governments have always lobbied to get their citizens appointed to senior positions within the UN. While UN staffers are technically neutral civil servants, it's no secret the primary loyalty of senior appointees usually lies with their national governments who ultimately decide how far they go in their international careers. It is virtually impossible to be appointed to a senior role in the UN without the support of your national government. Governments, meanwhile, want to have their citizens in strategic positions within the UN to be their eyes, ears and voices on the international stage. So, they often lobby to place one of their own in key positions when such become vacant. The outcomes of these lobbying battles tell a story about who wields influence in the UN at any given time.

A study analysing which countries' nationals occupied the most senior positions in the United Nations Secretariat over a sixty-year period following its inception, from 1947 to 2007, was quite revealing.[2] While the UN's Secretary General is the face of its decisions, the Secretariat is the brains behind them. It is responsible for the day-to-day running of the UN and manages its peacekeeping operations. It houses the Department of Political Affairs, which is the UN's equivalent of a foreign ministry, as well as its Department of Economic and Social Affairs, which crafts development policies.

It also plays a key role in setting the agenda for the UN's General Assembly and Security Council meetings. Agenda-setting is critical to influence, for as the House of Lords report put it, '*Gently* framing the international agenda can make other countries' preferences seem *irrelevant, illegitimate* or *unfeasible.*' Love the 'gently' bit, that's strategically subtle Britishness at its best for you.

The UN resolutions we hear about in the news usually originate in its Secretariat. The study revealed that the most over-represented countries in its senior cadres during that sixty-year period were all small white-majority nations – Finland, Sweden, Norway, New Zealand and Ireland. The researchers suggested 'diplomacy investment' was the chief reason for the outsized influence of these small nations. Diplomacy investment includes the number of embassies a country maintains in the world and the resources it devotes to strengthening its clout, be that via foreign aid or by wining and dining the high and mighty of this world at lavish diplomatic dos. Nordic countries like Sweden and Norway deploy the aid tool extensively. Norway's 2021 foreign aid budget[3] surpassed Rwanda's entire national budget.[4]

Most black and brown nations can't afford to devote significant resources to diplomatic clout-building. Nigeria has always been rightly described as the black nation with the greatest potential to become a global power and is one of the richest countries in Africa, yet its foreign missions are so chronically underfunded they sometimes struggle to meet rent on the buildings they occupy. Such situations constitute a 'terrible embarrassment' for the country, lamented Geoffrey Onyeama, Nigeria's foreign minister, in 2020.[5] '[As] the giant of Africa, we are supposed to defend the interest of Africa and the black race around the world . . . but Nigeria cannot get its international image to fit into the acceptable module of the international community if its foreign missions remain underfunded,' he observed.

During my time in Poland, I can't recall how many times I and other Nigerians in the country shook our heads bitterly at news that once again our embassy had been forced to relocate because it owed back-rent. Corruption was certainly a problem as significant chunks of the funds that were sent from Nigeria often ended up in the pockets of those at the top of the embassy food chain. But the funds were virtually always late in coming and what was allocated was an objectively small budget for an embassy representing the largest black nation on earth.

Other African missions face even bigger financial restrictions and their diplomats certainly don't have anything near the networking budgets Western diplomats do. African governments can hardly be blamed for not prioritising clout-building when they often struggle to meet basic domestic needs. But that doesn't change the answer to the unforgiving question of who is going to take seriously a nation whose embassies sometimes struggle to make rent? It's not as if these stories don't make it to the diplomatic grapevine.

We thus have the paradoxical situation in which a small Norway or Sweden can often wield more influence in the corridors of the UN than a big Nigeria. Other large non-white nations like India have also been traditionally under-represented in UN top positions. 'While Western countries' share of world population has been steadily declining since the creation of the United Nations, their control over the UN Secretariat has not wavered,' the study noted.

Again, I'm not saying this is *just* about money. Nordic bureaucrats benefit from popular perceptions of them as competent (again that word), trustworthy and neutral professionals. Nordic countries always do very well in national soft-power rankings and are widely seen as well-governed and equitable societies. Their nation brands are very strong, and this definitely helps in navigating the international arena.

Nevertheless, if they were seen as having these positive aspects but did not have the wherewithal for significant 'diplomatic investment' behind them, it is doubtful they would be so over-represented in the UN's senior ranks. Not to mention the fact that the positive national stereotypes Scandinavians enjoy in the first place are strongly connected to the economic success of their countries. That money plays a significant role in who gets influence at the UN is evidenced by the rapid progress China has made in increasing its clout there in recent years.

It has been able to successfully lobby for Chinese nationals to head a wide range of key agencies, ranging from the UN Food and Agriculture Organization to the International Telecommunication Union, crucial for its role in setting technical standards for global communications networks. In 2000, China contributed just 1 per cent of the UN's budget,[6] today it contributes 15 per cent, making it the second-largest contributor after the US.[7] In 2017, President Xi Jinping famously declared that China has entered a 'new era', one in which it would 'take centre stage in the world'. Its vastly increasing contributions to organisations like the UN are certainly helping this ambition.

The criteria for influence at the IMF, arguably the most important global financial institution in the world, are even more transparent. Thanks to rules set up at the wartime 1944 Bretton Woods conference dominated by the US and to a lesser extent Britain, each IMF member state is assigned a contributory quota, based on selected measures of a country's position in the world economy. A member's quota determines its voting share in IMF decisions, which basically means the more you pay, the more your say. The US makes the largest contribution to the IMF, giving it the largest single-country voting share of 17 per cent. Crucially, this means it is the only country with effective veto power over major IMF decisions, which often require an 85 per cent majority to pass.

Six of the top ten contributors and voting shareholders are white-majority nations.[8] The combined voting share of the high-income OECD bloc, which consists mostly of such nations, is 63 per cent.[9] The IMF's Executive Board, which is responsible for daily operations and appoints the IMF head, consists of twenty-four executive directors.[10] Membership on this board is also divided according to quotas. As a result, the highest contributing countries – the US, Britain, France, Germany, Russia, China, Japan and Saudi Arabia – each get a seat on the board while entire blocs of countries get to share a single seat. Sub-Saharan Africa, a region of forty-six nations, has just two executive directors representing its interests! Though the Americans control the largest voting share in the IMF, they have an informal arrangement with the Europeans in which the latter get to pick the head of the IMF while an American heads the World Bank. Since it was established in 1945, all IMF heads have been (white) Europeans.

The World Bank operates on a similar pay-to-play basis. Voting power is largely based on members' capital subscriptions.

Again, the US controls the largest voting share and rich, mostly Western countries generally dominate. Since its inception in 1944, every World Bank president has been an American citizen (a Bulgarian was Acting President for two months in 2019). Only two of these American World Bank heads have not been white – Jim Yong Kim, and most recently, Ajaypal Banga, who was appointed in 2023.

I emphasise the racial group of the World Bank and IMF heads not out of an unhealthy obsession with skin colour but because, aside from the formal economic powers those who run these institutions (and those who get to pick those who run them) wield, they also wield immense psychological power.

People around the world will often see on their evening news when a sitting World Bank or IMF head visits their country. That person will usually meet with their president or prime minister. And if the World Bank or IMF head is visiting your country, it's likely your government needs money. Some loan or development aid of some kind or the other. Thus, the situational context in which people will absorb these images is one of the powerful white person who can push the Yes or No decision on whether their usually black or brown nation will receive financial assistance or not. The message to black and brown people around the world is clear: white people control the money. Which means they control the world. This builds the position of white people in the minds of billions of other people around the world. Power is best perpetuated by perceptions of it. The World Bank and IMF are undoubtedly hierarchy-enhancing institutions when it comes to the racial ordering of this world.

These IMF and World Bank rules were of course set up in 1944, back when white nations completely dominated the global economy. Things have changed somewhat since then, and today China especially, but also some of the other wealthier nations of the global South, could easily afford to buy themselves more voting power in the IMF and World Bank. But the Western bloc does not want to relinquish control of those institutions which are vital to maintaining its status in the global hierarchy, and consequently derail such attempts.

Crucially, they still have more than enough financial muscle to be able to finance the IMF and World Bank with or without Chinese or any other non-Western money, which pretty much checkmates the latter nations. Money gives you lots of leverage with the poor, less so with the rich. Because Western nations are still very wealthy, they can afford to maintain a tight grip on the IMF and World Bank irrespective of the economic rise of some non-Western nations. A realisation of this is one of the reasons China decided to set up its own alternative 'World Bank', the Asian Infrastructure Investment Bank, while the BRICS countries – Brazil, Russia, India, China and South Africa – together established the New Development Bank. The Asian Infrastructure Investment Bank (AIIB) is the bigger player today with over a hundred member countries.

Pragmatic as ever, several Western powers like Britain, France, Germany and Australia have joined the AIIB, where they again have larger voting shares than most of the black and brown nations.[11] Because the rules there too remain pretty much the same – pay to play. Only difference is this time it is China that has reserved itself permanent control of the institution with a voting share that gives it de facto veto power over major decisions. Which is why the US has of course steadfastly refused to join the AIIB and was quite upset with the likes of Britain for doing so, as it obviously doesn't like any arrangement that strengthens China's global position.

But the AIIB is still a long way from achieving the kind of influence the IMF and World Bank enjoy, considering they've been around for nearly eighty years now and are household names across the world. People in remote villages have heard of the IMF and World Bank. Paradoxically, the legends that have grown around these institutions thanks to their detractors ascribing them near omnipotent powers of influence in the global economy have only strengthened their position. Thanks to the countless articles, books and speeches that have been focused on them, these institutions have attained near mythical status. And that is exactly the kind of status power needs.

To be clear, it is difficult to imagine that if the largest contributors to the World Bank, IMF or UN today were, say, black nations, they would not seek to have more influence on its decision-making processes than others. Let's not be hypocritical. Of course they would, just as China has engineered itself control of the Asian Infrastructure Investment Bank and is actively expanding its influence wherever it can at the moment. It is also using its muscle within the UN to slow down the rise of other ascending non-Western states; for instance, it is actively blocking India from becoming a fellow Permanent Member of the UN Security Council. 'China is biggest stumbling block in India's UNSC permanent membership,' complained the *Hindustan Times* in 2020.[12] Institutions are a reflection of the distribution of power in the world and the struggles to *redistribute* that power. That struggle is inescapable because power gives you agency, and who doesn't want agency?

The problem is not that today's white Westerners are somehow inherently more power-oriented than other human beings. The problem is that they still have way too much power relative to others. They have too much of a capacity to dominate the global institutions that structure the world. This makes for more than an uneven international playing field, it makes for what is, if we're being honest, very often a rigged game. One in which the players already know who will win before the whistle is blown, but just go through the motions for the benefit of the rest of us, so they are not accused of not trying.

Psychologically, they create environments in which poorer less powerful nations and the racial groups that inhabit them are constantly reminded of their lower position in the global hierarchy. Observers of international trade negotiations have noted how African delegations often have to resort to a 'Crying Game' strategy during such meetings.[13] Because Africa accounts for just 3 per cent of global trade, African governments face a perpetually uphill struggle trying to win favourable trade terms with, say the EU, which accounts for 16 per cent of global trade.

Hence, they often emphasise the difficulty of their economic situations, stressing how much poverty there is in their countries and how badly they need economic development in order to try to improve the terms they are offered. This sometimes yields some results but at the cost of emphasising the weakness of their positions. And even if just subconsciously, delegates from say a Kenya or a Bangladesh will be regularly comparing the strength of their voice in the UN et al with the strength of voices from a Germany or a Canada. And they will be constantly reminded that the latter's voices weigh much more internationally.

As a Nigerian government official said to me, 'At international conferences on issues like climate change, global finance or global health governance, those of us in African delegations often have many ideas for solutions. We come with our presentations, we cite our statistics and make our arguments. The white delegations listen and nod politely. But then at the end of all our speeches and presentations, one question always pops up. Who will pay for all this? At that point, we in the African delegations usually fall silent while those who have the money start talking, proposing *their* solutions, the ones that best serve *their* interests. And in the end, though some little concessions are usually made to us here and there so we can save face and have something to present back home, it is ultimately their solutions that almost always carry the day. For in the end, we are left with a simple choice: it is either their solutions or no solutions at all.'

And as Vladimir Putin brutally reminded us in 2022, if militarily strong nations don't get the outcomes they want via diplomacy or financial leverage, they *can* ultimately resort to their hard power. Even if countries with significant hard power don't bring it up in interactions with other nations, it is always there, lurking in the background of their attitudes and the attitudes of others towards them. Military might will continue to be a major power provider for the foreseeable future because when it boils down to it, the ultimate leverage you can wield over human beings is the power to kill them. And when it comes to possessing this kind of power on a large scale, it is again predominantly white nations who hold the advantage. One they have wielded on more than one occasion in recent history.

In a 2006 interview, Pakistan's president Pervez Musharraf told CBS News that the George W. Bush administration threatened to bomb his country 'back to the Stone Age' if Pakistan did not cooperate with America's war in Afghanistan following the September 11 terrorist attacks.[14] Musharraf said the message was delivered by then assistant US Secretary of State, Richard Armitage, to Pakistan's intelligence director. The leader of the fifth-largest nation in the world said he was stunned at the bluntness of the threat. But he had little choice than to yield to Washington's 'request' for cooperation. Indeed, what else was he to do in the face of someone with the capacity to virtually obliterate his country?

And this was Pakistan, a country which has nuclear weapons, though, crucially, not the kind that can reach US cities. If Washington knew Pakistan had nuclear missiles that could effectively target and destroy entire American cities, they would likely have been more diplomatic with Islamabad. But as of today, only five nations in the world can hit any place on earth with a nuclear missile: Russia, the US, China, France and Britain.[15] It is no coincidence it is these countries that are the five permanent members of the UN Security Council.

There's no harder power than military power, which gives you the capacity not just to attack nations but to offer them protection from attacks by others, as America offers the likes of Japan, South Korea and Taiwan in Asia, making itself their indispensable ally thanks to these countries' fears of China. The reason why key white-majority nations have so much more hard power in comparison to others is because the deadliest weapons cost a ton of money to produce and procure. America spent $801 billion on its military in 2021 alone.[16] Britain spent

$68 billion, Russia $66 billion, France $57 billion, Germany $56 billion, and Japan $54 billion. Not a single black nation was in the top 40 spenders.

Asia is the only non-Western region where some countries have recently started devoting major resources to boosting their military strength, with China and India predictably leading the way, spending $293 billion and $77 billion respectively in 2021. Suffice to say many Western nations are going to significantly ramp up military spending following the bitter experience of Putin's actions in Ukraine. In response to his aggression, Germany has already allocated an extra €100 billion to upgrade its army. So, we can expect to see several white-majority nations that have been spending a lot on their armies for centuries now, increase their hard power even more in the coming years. They certainly have the resources for it.

The reality today is that while the likes of China and India have pretty much ensured they could never again be conquered by white folk, Africa has not. A handful of the strongest Western military powers could today bomb the continent 'back to the Stone Age' if they so decided. Its existing air-defences would be virtually helpless against the kind of air power at Western disposal, to say nothing of the countless missiles in their arsenals. The fact that Africa remains so vulnerable a century and a half after the 1884 Berlin conference carved it up between European powers is a huge disadvantage in the racial dynamic.

Black nations need strong armies capable of projecting hard power. In terms of a power balance, it is paradoxically unfortunate that South Africa's then apartheid government gave up its nuclear programme in the early 1990s after successfully assembling six nuclear weapons.[17] Apartheid was an inherently untenable arrangement due to South Africa's demographics, so holding on to those weapons wouldn't have saved the system anyway. And if the government of the day had held on to them, there would now be at least one black-led nation with nuclear weapons. Since others have them, at least one or two black nations should too.

None of this makes much sense at a deeper level. Billions being spent on armies and crazy weapons of all sorts when there's so much poverty and hunger in the world? In 2021, global military spending stood at $2.1 trillion. It is estimated it would cost six times less – $330 billion – to *end* world hunger by 2030.[18] Yet I suspect that by 2030, hunger will still be with us while military spending will be way above $2 trillion. Not because many human beings are against ending world hunger, but because it takes just one country to start an arms race. Others join out of fear. It's either nobody wants arms or everybody wants arms. What would need to happen for us to live in a world in which *nobody* wants arms?

It would take pretty much all of us, not just a few people here and there, fundamentally changing the way we think about ourselves and each other. It would require us instinctively trusting each other whether we share the same skin colour, religion, ethnicity, nationality, ideologies and values or not. It would require us being able to consistently separate the fearful thoughts and emotions in our heads from the external world around us.

It would require us viewing ourselves and the groups we identify with not as separate sovereign entities but as mutually conditioned parts of a larger whole. It would require all of us feeling a sense of responsibility towards everyone else in the world, which would mean ignoring the regular advice of our individual and collective egos that we need first and foremost to look out for ourselves and *our kind*. It would require an internal transformation in pretty much all of us. Comparing what we are today to what we were a thousand years ago, are there grounds to believe this is possible? Some grounds, certainly.

The way the world 'works' has changed in very many aspects over the past few centuries and I think it's clear we live in much better, less brutal realities than those our ancestors had to endure centuries ago. I personally consider myself very lucky for having been born in the twentieth, not the tenth century. We humans are unfinished products and definitely evolving in a better direction. I suspect those living in the thirtieth century will be living in a better world than we are today. Nothing is a given, and certainly nothing is a given forever. History suggests our agency is real, however constrained.

Nevertheless, the capitalist system we inhabit today conditions us to be even more egoistic and hierarchical in our thinking than we would be by natural inclination, and those inclinations themselves are strong. Various versions of communism and socialism have been practised in various parts of the world in recent history, none of which seemed to make the humans living in those systems significantly less egoistic, fearful, hierarchical or willing to commit violence against other humans.

Last century, millions of people were killed in the name of communism, which was supposed to make us less egoistic, more egalitarian beings. In practice, one of the most striking aspects of communism was how strongly hierarchical it was, with its powerful party secretaries, central committees and almost always one *man* sitting atop everyone else, be it Josef

Stalin, Fidel Castro or Chairman Mao. Always a pecking order, always some person or group dominating others. Clearly, we have not yet created or even imagined a functional socio-economic system that would foster the mass internal transformation needed for us to create a world without *more thans* and *less thans*. Hopefully, someone somewhere will think up such a system one day. I wish I were clever enough to be that person, but alas.

So for the world we have today at our current stage of human evolution, a dynamic in which predominantly white countries enjoy an overwhelming hard power advantage over most black and brown nations is not a healthy dynamic. For the latter, there is always the danger, however minimal, that this advantage could be used against them at some point, even if in a mere moment of madness. To have to rely on the restraint of others for your safety is not a good position to be in. Neither is this a healthy dynamic for the minds of those with significant hard power, for the temptation to use an available means at your disposal to achieve an end you desire can overcome even the most restrained or best intentioned of us at times.

A world where nations, and by extension the racial groups that dominate them, do not compete for (more) global power appears unlikely for now. In fact, according to the UK government's 2021 Integrated Review of Security, Defence, Development and Foreign Policy, the next decade will be defined by 'the intensification of competition between states'. The mere expectation of such competition will itself perpetuate it.

Some will focus on competing economically, technologically and diplomatically, in other words, non-violently. Yet others who may feel less competitive in these spheres but stronger in the military sphere might prefer to focus on that arena of competition. Russia's actions in Ukraine were a good example of this. Bottom line is, whatever the choice of competitive focus, money will be needed to fuel it. The wealth situation of today thus places most black and brown nations at a distinct disadvantage going forward in the global arena. The old maxim that the strong do what they can and the weak suffer what they must still applies to international politics today. There is, however, one significant countertrend to this arguably male-centric vision of the world and its future that is worth discussing in its racial context – the feminisation of power in the West. Let us now move on to this quite fascinating and consequential development

9

The feminisation of white power

In 2015, Marlon James, the Man Booker Prize winner for that year, caused a storm in the publishing world when he said authors of colour 'too often pander to white women' to sell books.[1] James, who is Jamaican and whose first novel was rejected by publishers seventy-eight times, said 'if I pandered to a cultural tone set by white women, particularly older white female critics, I would have had ten stories published by now'.

While authors of colour have been criticising the publishing industry for a while, what made James' words provoke such a strong reaction, aside from his high profile, was the fact he had highlighted the power of white *women* in that world. Most authors of colour usually restrict themselves to generalised complaints about the whiteness of the industry, so as not to alienate its indeed powerful white females who, in addition to being able to decide a writing career, often present themselves as allies in the struggle against a common enemy – the arrogant white male.

Nevertheless, a survey conducted a year after James' comments found that 79 per cent of those working in the US publishing industry were white and 78 per cent were female.[2] Those figures lent his criticisms new weight, reigniting the debate over an industry that has the power to popularise stories on a global scale. Promises were made to diversify the US publishing workforce. But when the survey was repeated in 2020, its demographics had barely budged.[3] Likewise, a 2020 survey of the UK publishing industry revealed it to be overwhelmingly white female.[4]

Again, money plays a significant role here. Five of the six biggest book markets in the world are white-majority countries – the US, Germany, UK, France and Italy.[5] Surveys show women account for 80 per cent of sales in the US and UK fiction markets.[6] Most of these book-buyers are *white* women. The commercial reasons for publishers and writers 'pandering' to the white Western female reader are thus pretty evident. The sheer size of Western book markets, both in fiction and non-fiction, is the chief reason the ten biggest publishing houses in the world in terms of revenue in 2021 were all either European or North American.[7] The 'Big Four' publishing houses that dominate the global market – Penguin Random House, Macmillan, Hachette Book Group (whose imprint Little, Brown are the publishers of this book) and HarperCollins – are all Western-based and owned.

So, just like with universities and media, when we speak of '*the* publishing industry' in a global sense, what we are really talking about is the Western publishing industry. Suffice to say, none of the major global publishing houses are owned and controlled by black or brown people. There is not a single

Africa-based or black-owned publishing company among the top fifty publishers.

In an ideal world, a Nigerian or Indian writer, especially if based in their country, shouldn't have to care what the racial make-up of the workforce of an American or British publishing house is. Because there'd be Nigerian and Indian publishers with the ability to promote their work internationally. But while there are publishing companies all over the world doing great work trying to promote writers, their marketing, distribution and prestige-conferring capacities are significantly restricted. The resources at their disposal are puny compared to what the Western behemoths control. Most home-based African writers, even those who are fairly well known, have to rely on self-publishing models to get their work out, which means *they* pay for their books to be published and then hope they recover their investment in sales. That is the reality for writers in most parts of the world.

It is why the best-known black and brown writers usually choose to be published by white-controlled Western publishing houses rather than by existent but much smaller black and brown-owned publishing houses around the world. As in the case of Western media, if a black or brown writer wants to reach an international audience, they usually have to go through a Western publishing house. And that is no easy task, considering they are competing with white writers who editors often believe have readier audiences in the most lucrative predominantly white book markets.

A *New York Times* investigation found that 95 per cent of the English-language fiction books published by the major publishing houses between 1950 and 2018 were by white authors.[8] In the most recent year examined – 2018 – the figure was still a whopping 89 per cent. At the time of the survey, the heads of all the 'big four' publishing houses were white.

News cycles and intellectual trends usually determine how many authors of colour get published by the major players. One unintended consequence of the 2020 murder of George Floyd was that black people and racism suddenly became hot news. In June 2020, during the peak of the Black Lives Matter protests following Floyd's killing, all of the top ten books on the *New York Times* non-fiction bestseller list were about racism, including titles like *So You Want to Talk About Race* by Ijeoma Oluo, *How to Be an Antiracist* by Ibram X. Kendi, and *Me and White Supremacy* by Layla F. Saad. Meanwhile, Reni Eddo-Lodge's *Why I'm No Longer Talking to White People about Race* was the bestselling book on Amazon here in the UK.

During such periods, publishers will rush to put out books by black authors. But once the uproar has died down and the hashtags have stopped trending, it's usually a return to the status quo of focusing on whatever content they believe their bulk Western audiences, white females especially, will be most interested in reading.

This is not to say that white female readers may not be colour blind in their choice of who to read. Even more, they may sometimes *want* to read books by authors of colour who have different perspectives from those they usually encounter in their everyday lives. An industry source told me most of the books on racism that have gone on to become bestsellers in recent years are also primarily bought by white females. This brings us to the wider racial implications of the growing influence of white women not just in the publishing world but in many key spheres of Western society.

Like at any time in history, there are several ongoing group struggles in the Western world today. Two are of particular relevance for us. On the one hand, the West's racial minorities are engaged in a struggle to wrest some power for themselves from the white majority. On the other, there is a power tussle ongoing within that white majority, that between its two main sexes.

Of course, groups with less power usually don't say they're fighting for more power but for *equality*. Phrasing it that way helps draw on the substantial public sympathy often accruing to the underdog and provokes less resistance among those powerful enough to block whatever change is sought. But what is going on today *is* a struggle for power and that is nothing to be shy about. When we hear the word 'power', we too often think of situations in which one person literally holds the life chances of another in their hands. Reality is usually less dramatic than that. Power in day-to-day life is simply the ability to have some meaningful influence on the people and things affecting your destiny as an individual or collective.

You need power to have agency in this world and no one should be shy about wanting some. There's no reason why some groups should have plenty of power while others just sit and observe them enjoying its benefits. Suffice to say, we are all engaged in power tussles with each other, most of which are conducted in a perfectly peaceful and friendly fashion and end in some greater or lesser compromise. And then we move on till the next tussle, or 'negotiation' if you prefer. There is nothing sinister about any of this as a rule, though it can of course *become* sinister when it gets out of hand and power stops being pursued as a means to an end but as an end in and of itself.

While men still dominate most of the powerful positions in the West, women are clearly on the ascendant in many influential spheres, ranging from media and academia to government institutions and corporations. The past few decades have witnessed one of the most dramatic cultural changes the West has seen in recorded history, the shift towards gender equality and increasing female influence in public life. Crucially, it is now women who are increasingly setting the tone for how we *should* speak and act in the public sphere. Especially in the workplace where we spend a significant chunk of our lives and where important aspects of our destinies are shaped.

A key reason 'equality', 'diversity' and 'inclusivity' have become standard staples of Western public speak is because women dominate the upper echelons of Human Resource departments, which decide and enforce norms of communication and behaviour in organisations. Sixty-seven percent of the Human Resources directors in FTSE 100 companies are women.[9] HR is also a female-dominated profession in America.[10]

The power to set the tone for how we speak and act in public is a significant one as it leads to influence on how power is exercised in practice. Female influence has led to power in the West today presenting itself way more discreetly than it used to, with a smile (sincere or not), a sympathetic air and a general emphasis on empathy over obedience. This is not a coincidence.

Social Dominance Theory (SDT), which was developed by social psychologists to explain how human hierarchies are established and maintained, has shown that individuals and nations vary in their attitudes to hierarchies, some being more instinctively supportive of them, others much less so. One survey of twenty-seven nations found Poles, Russians, Hungarians, Romanians and Serbians displaying significantly higher levels of support for societal hierarchies than Germans, Swedes, Spaniards, Italians or Dutch.[11] The Japanese were the most domination-oriented while the Taiwanese, Chinese and Indians showed a similar fondness for hierarchies to Eastern Europeans.

Of the nations surveyed, the Swiss were the least domination-oriented, perhaps a legacy of their unique system of direct democracy which entrenches egalitarian values. Indeed, the strongest predictor of a society's support for hierarchies was how entrenched egalitarian values were within it. The more entrenched, the less domination-oriented it was. However, it isn't just enough for a society to talk about egalitarian values, what is key is that citizens *believe* they are feasible. This is more easily the case in societies that are not radically unequal to start with. People talk about equality in Nigeria, but most Nigerians deep down don't believe it is feasible because equality sounds like a pipe dream in a society where some have everything and others literally nothing. Neither does societal wealth alone determine attitudes towards domination. Japan and Taiwan have both been well-off for decades yet exhibit strong support for hierarchies. It is the combination of prosperity *and* an emphasis on egalitarianism that can reduce the hierarchical thinking we are imbued with from our earliest years.

Studies also show that men are generally more domination-oriented than women. While the origin of this difference is a matter of debate among psychologists, with some pointing to evolutionary adaptation and others to gendered social identities, what has been evidenced is that there *is* a difference in how men and women approach domination. When this was first noticed, researchers set out to test whether the difference was affected by age, political ideology, attitude to abortion rights, religion, culture, ethnicity, education, income level or racial group membership.

A major study was conducted on a large group of adults living in Los Angeles but hailing from various cultural regions – the US, Europe, Canada, South America, Asia and the Middle East.[12] Across cultures, men were consistently found to be more domination-oriented than women. Whether the women were conservative or liberal, religious or secular, white or brown, pro-abortion or anti-abortion, well-educated or not, they were, as a rule, less domination-oriented than their male counterparts. Similar surveys in countries where the everyday situation of women varies significantly – China, the US, Israel, Palestine and New Zealand – confirmed this trend. As did an analysis of attitudes among over fifty thousand respondents gleaned from 206 samples and 118 independent reports.[13]

Men are the most frequent perpetrators of intergroup violence, which is usually aimed at asserting control or outright domination. Historically, collective violence, ranging from military and gang wars to lynchings, has been almost exclusively instigated, organised and controlled by men. Men are not only the primary perpetrators of intergroup violence, they usually target other males. Between 1882 and 1927, 69 per cent of black lynching victims in the US were men.[14]

It is believed this different attitude towards domination is one of the reasons men are often drawn to careers in institutions that tend to *enhance* societal hierarchies, such as the police, the army, the criminal justice system, or the corporate world. Women, meanwhile, are over-represented in roles that serve to *attenuate* societal hierarchies: as teachers, social workers, charity volunteers and the like. While women are sometimes discriminated *out of* the hierarchy-enhancing professions men tend to like being in control of, they do often *choose* to work in hierarchy-attenuating occupations and institutions. They are generally more supportive of social equality, inclusive norms, and policies tending to shield the most vulnerable.

As a result of today's increasing female influence in Western societies, the traditional strongman leadership model is increasingly being replaced by a focus on people skills and emotional intelligence. The ability to effectively project empathy is slowly but surely replacing the ability to coerce obedience as the chief leadership skill in the West. And I'm not just talking among lefties.

It is no coincidence that centre-right conservative parties like the Tories, who used to pride themselves on their toughness – even under female leaders like Thatcher – are now no longer comfortable playing bad cop and being seen as endorsing hierarchies. Boris Johnson's government wanted a 'levelling up' of Britain; in other words, a flattening of its hierarchies.

Levelling up might not be the key slogan of Rishi Sunak's government, but the general language of most frontline Tory politicians has changed significantly from what it used to be, in the direction of a greater emphasis on fairness, equality etc. The motivations behind this are less important than the fact their polling strategists have obviously told them this is the way to be popular in the twenty-first century. Many people today want more of caring mummy than tough-it-out daddy. Societal expectations of power have changed dramatically in the West.

I believe one of the reasons Trump was so unpalatable to so many in this part of the world was because he was constantly breaking the new rules of power etiquette many now hold dear. Today's Westerner is most comfortable enjoying their society's accumulated wealth and power without being reminded how much more of it they have than people elsewhere. They prefer leaders who obscure the reality of Western power with smiles and respectful rhetoric towards the poor and the weak, even if these amount to mere platitudes. 'We treat everyone respectfully,' today's Westerners want to be able to say of themselves. Most are no longer comfortable with their leaders openly lording it over others.

Trump, meanwhile, tried to reassert a hyper-masculine version of white power. One which essentially said 'What's all this equality nonsense? *We* have all the power, why on earth should we care what all these nobody groups think? On the contrary, we need to remind them who runs this world!' This approach did of course appeal to quite a lot of Americans, considering the tens of millions who still voted for him in 2020, including some non-whites, Hispanics especially, who clearly appreciate his style. There is definitely some serious push-back to the feminisation of Western power.

Here in Europe, it has perhaps been most clearly articulated by the hard-right 2022 French presidential candidate Éric Zemmour, who wrote a bestselling book titled *The French Suicide*. Zenmour complains Frenchmen are being socialised into a culture that increasingly elevates feminine values. 'If power does not stay in men's hands, it fades away,' he argues.[15] He predicts France is heading towards a future in which white Frenchmen who are now too feminine will soon, along with white French women, be shoved aside by macho brown Muslim men in France who have retained their masculine desire to dominate. Because, as Zenmour argues, outside Western cultures, men defend their dominant status 'like a treasure'.[16]

I've heard similar takes from many right-wing Polish male commentators in recent years. It reflects a fear among some white men that the increasing influence of women in shaping what is seen as acceptable behaviour from power here in the West will lead to a world in which whites lose their power altogether. They fear white feminists are attacking the authority of the white male so effectively that they are naively creating a power void which macho black and brown men will soon step in to fill, replacing them as the dominant actors of our world.

As a man who was brought up in a very macho culture, I get where this kind of thinking comes from. And I do agree many white Western men appear not quite sure who they are or want to be today and are constantly searching for external validation as to whether their behaviour is appropriate or not. With the economic dependency of women on men effectively now history in the West, many Western men are clearly no longer sure what their role in the big picture is any more. Hence the huge popularity of thinkers like Jordan Peterson, who have stepped in to provide a guiding hand to confused young males.

It is likewise correct to say that in most places outside the West, men do defend their dominant status 'like a treasure' and unabashed patriarchy tends to be the norm. A litmus test for opinions about gender roles is usually the question of whether men make better political leaders than women. The 2022 World Values Survey revealed that in the world as a whole, a majority still believe men make better political leaders than women with the figure as high as 75 per cent in Nigeria and Pakistan while over half of Russians, Turks, Indonesians and South Koreans feel this way too.[17]

In comparison, 16 per cent of Americans, 12 per cent of Australians and 8 per cent of Germans share this bias, which is being rejected by growing majorities in the West and most resolutely by younger generations. So it is true that men elsewhere still tend to consider themselves destined to run the show and actively block women from having a greater say in things. However, the fear of a black or brown male takeover of the West is paranoia, to say the least.

Moreover, it's a paranoia that has been around since way before the feminisation of power in the West. Such fears seem to have been present in white men even when an entire system of slavery existed to ensure their domination! But more recently, the Conservative politician Enoch Powell's infamous 'Rivers of Blood' speech predicted that 'the black man will soon have the whip hand over the white man' here in Britain.[18] This was in 1968, well before feminism became a powerful force.

Suffice to say, the black man is hardly holding the whip hand over the white man today, more than half a century after that forecast. On the contrary, one thing we have learnt since then and which seems to have escaped Zenmour et al is that a capitalist world is ruled by money, not machismo. Considering nothing on the ground suggests black or brown men are suddenly going to come into control of the West's vast wealth, fears they will somehow start dominating white men here in Europe because they have retained their 'masculinity' are rather fanciful. If it were that easy.

The feminisation trend in the West *has* been a strategic positive for racial minorities as it has helped delegitimise the use of overt aggression and intimidation in the exercise of power. Not just towards minorities, of course, but generally speaking. In most Western societies, it is no longer socially acceptable to openly lord it over those you have more power than. You in fact have to be quite careful not to be seen as abusing your power, especially if you are a white male. This is something we seem to take for granted now but it is a massive shift in attitude compared to the realities those who came before us had to endure.

If we view the world through the Chinese concept of yin and yang, which claims that the world is constantly being pulled by contradictory, yet inseparable energy forces, such as male (yang) and female (yin), then we can say the West is currently being pulled in a yin direction more strongly than ever in history. By enshrining equality and inclusivity as value norms, Western power structures have, at the very least, opened themselves up for critique if they fail to live up to the standards they now swear by.

If not for the increasing feminisation of power in the West, I doubt even the rhetoric of racial equality would be as commonplace as it is now, not to speak of the practice of it.

If this part of the world was still dominated by men like it was fifty years ago, I have little doubt the racial hierarchy would be more aggressively imposed than it is today. That tends to be the male instinct, and not just the white male instinct. If black people as a group wielded significantly more wealth and power than others, there would likely be many black men wanting to maintain a global hierarchy with them at the top. This tends to be the way men would have it if they could.

Nevertheless, even a more benign feminised version of white power does not change the fundamental reality of the status quo. In the publishing world discussed earlier on, it is a reality in which authors of colour may often have to skew their stories towards appealing to white female sensibilities if they want to make a living selling books. It is a reality in which too many people of colour in too many professions remain similarly dependent on the opinions, tastes and caprices of white people, male and female, in order to thrive. Such dependence helps sustain the racial hierarchy. As does the fact that the power to allocate global prestige in the spheres of culture and entertainment likewise remains in mostly white hands.

What made Marlon James' words about authors of colour having to pander to white female tastes really matter was that he enjoyed the prestige of being a Booker Prize winner. The Booker Prize is a British primarily white-funded prize given out by the Booker Foundation. All creative professions have their own version of *the* award that can change your life overnight. Actors around the world dream of winning an Oscar, which is an American award. Musicians dream of a Grammy, also an American award. Few writers even dare dream of winning the Nobel Prize in Literature, which is decided by a Swedish academy. For journalists, the career changer is the Pulitzer Prize (American). For photographers, it's the World Press Photo, which is awarded by a foundation based in Amsterdam.

Virtually all *the* creative awards the world is familiar with and most in awe of are allocated in the predominantly white Western world. White Westerners thus still control the allocation of global esteem in the cultural sphere. No award given in any other part of the world comes even close to competing with the ones mentioned in prestige value. Winning any of these awards I've mentioned makes you an instant *global* 'somebody'.

If you didn't already have an army of followers on social media, you will after such a decision has been announced. Your mere presence at events will start meaning something anywhere in the world. Your observations on your craft and even things unrelated will suddenly gain more weight, be seen as insightful and relevant. In short, you will suddenly be quite a big deal in the world's eyes.

Most Nigerians are more impressed by the Nigerian artiste who's won, say, a Grammy, than another who may have won several Nigerian or African awards, but no *Western* ones. The black or brown writer with a Nobel Prize is treated like royalty in their home country because they have been recognised as brilliant by, let's face it, *white people*. In contrast, there is not a single creative award handed out in a black or brown dominion that is considered globally prestigious. Again, when we talk about 'international' awards in the creative industry, what we really mean are Western awards. It is folly to imagine one can eliminate a hierarchy headed by a particular group if their members are the chief allocators of prestige and fortune in so many spheres of our cultural life.

10

Moral power

There is power in morality. To emphasise the role of the material is not to deny that. People can wield significant moral power over others, as can ideas. Moral power is the degree to which a person or idea is able to persuade people of the *right way* to think and behave. Martin Luther King Jnr's call for an America in which people 'will not be judged by the colour of their skin but by the content of their character' has been quoted countless times as a foundational premise for racial equality, attaining an almost constitution-like status. In this case, both the person and the idea continue to wield huge moral sway, hence it is regularly evoked by people on various sides of the race debate, from right to left, to support their arguments.

'Clearly the leader who commands compelling causes has an extraordinary potential influence over followers,' as US political scientist James Burns observed in his seminal book *Leadership*.[1] However, in people's everyday lives, they rarely come face to face with historical leaders. It is, rather, those around them who have the greatest influence on their daily behaviour.

When someone says we need to do X because it is 'the right thing to do' that person is attempting to influence our actions with an appeal to morality. Parents often use this argument in trying to encourage certain behaviour in their children, as do politicians and other influence-seekers wishing to persuade us to their ideas. There is never a shortage of people and ideas that wish to persuade us how the world *should* work. Those we find most persuasive attain moral power.

In religious, very family-oriented societies like Nigeria and many others in the global South, pastors, imams and other spiritual leaders hold significant sway over many, as do family members, especially older ones. Deference to their moral advice is considered a virtue while defiance of it is frowned upon and seen to be a sign of badness. In contrast, Western nations pride themselves on being secular, rational societies where individual autonomy is prioritised over religion, traditional family values and obedience to moral authorities. In practice, however, moral power can be every bit as difficult to defy in the West as anywhere else.

People find it difficult to challenge ideas or people with moral power in the environment they operate in. They will rather disagree silently than openly. Few things daunt *Homo sapiens* more than the prospect of social ostracism. It doesn't feel nice to be a pariah and it is difficult to thrive anywhere if people decide to shun you. And they *will* do this to you if you defy the moral worldviews they have adopted. Saying you think homosexuality should be criminalised would make you a pariah in today's Britain, as the idea everyone should enjoy sexual freedom has attained significant moral power here. In other places, coming out as gay would make you a pariah as the idea homosexuality is wrong has attained great moral power in those societies. People are thus careful about what they say and do around others. They are constantly sniffing the moral atmosphere around them to sense where the winds are blowing, especially on issues people feel strongly about, such as race.

Following the Holocaust and other atrocities committed by the Nazis in the Second World War, it became clear to most white thought-leaders that *overt* racism was no longer morally defensible. In the late 1940s, the African American writer W.E.B Du Bois noted how Hitler's racism towards other *Europeans* had alerted white people to the dangers of the kind of extreme chauvinism they'd felt comfortable subjecting non-whites to for centuries.

The Zimbabwean scholar Sabelo Ndlovu-Gatsheni described how the post-Hitler reassessment of racism provided the opening for Africans to challenge colonialism in their lands.[2] 'The struggles for decolonization proceeded as claims for the inclusion of Africans in the post-1945 normative order. The Universal Declaration of Human Rights of 1948 was closely studied by African freedom fighters and its linguistic inventories were used to put pressure on Europe to decolonize Africa,' wrote Ndlovu-Gatsheni. What 'linguistic inventories' was he referring to?

The 1948 Universal Declaration of Human Rights, adopted by the UN General Assembly, started by asserting, 'All human beings are born free and equal in dignity and rights.'[3] It then added, crucially for those living in colonies, that 'everyone is entitled to all the rights and freedoms set forth in this Declaration, without distinction of any kind, such as race, colour, sex, language, religion, political or other opinion, national or social origin . . . Furthermore, no distinction shall be made on the basis of the political, jurisdictional or international status of the country or territory to which a person belongs, whether it be independent, trust, non-self-governing or under any other limitation of sovereignty.'

At a time when much of the world was under colonial rule, this was a game-changing moment in the race debate, one with significant practical consequences. Pro-independence leaders in Africa and Asia could now say to their colonial overlords: You have declared you believe in human equality and freedom for all; *prove it* by leaving us to enjoy the same freedoms you enjoy.

Having signed up to these declarations, countries like Britain could no longer defend colonialism as being in any way *right*. All they had left were technocratic arguments that their colonies were not ready for the practicalities of self-government and required some more time to prepare. But they were now on the moral defensive and most people find that an uncomfortable position to be in psychologically.

Moral arguments matter because they are often the only weapon of the (materially) weak. They played a significant role in ending colonialism and the Trans-Atlantic slave trade by ultimately rendering both embarrassingly difficult for white people to defend. While in some colonies, the independence struggle involved armed uprisings such as the Mau Mau rebellion in Kenya, in others like Nigeria, the decolonisation process boiled down to one long negotiation between the British and its pro-independence leaders.

One of those leaders, Obafemi Awolowo, often emphasised that Nigerian independence was won 'without firing a single shot' but by a combination of mass mobilisation and moral persuasion. His movement's message to Britain had been simple: Colonial rule does not meet the moral standards you profess to practise. It is an unfair system you, a people who proclaim their fairness at every turn, have imposed. How do you square that contradiction?

Britain eventually had to acknowledge it could not be squared and the strategic thing to do was leave. 'Strategic' because the powerful know that maintaining some level of moral authority is helpful in reducing potential resistance when they do decide to deploy their material power. The British knew resisting Nigerian independence for too long risked hostility to their economic interests in a post-colonial Nigeria that was going to come anyway. Best to leave while they still maintained some moral credibility, 'goodwill' as British officials called it, with Nigerians. Even the most powerful strive to appear moral to garner goodwill, as while it is not countable, it is bankable. America, the most powerful country in the world, consistently presents itself as a nation driven by *values*. US leaders don't go around saying 'We have power,' they say, 'We have values.' In other words, we have a moral code, we are good people with good intentions.

This strategic need of the powerful to maintain some level of moral authority creates an opportunity weaker parties can leverage in their dealings with them. The US civil rights movement didn't have fighter jets or a bigger budget than America's white establishment. But they had arguments that won them moral power. These arguments were summed up in

MLK's 1963 'I have a dream' speech, cited earlier, calling for people to be judged by the content of their character, an appeal to the Christian values white America professed to live by.

Major events can create new moral powers or strengthen existing ones. The latter happened following the 2020 killing of George Floyd by a white police officer. The widely circulated video of the killing convinced many hitherto neutral Americans that Black Lives Matter and other antiracist activists had been right all along on how to think of race in America. Simply put, white America was racist. This boost in moral power helped BLM mobilise mass protests in the US and elsewhere around the world.

From Washington to London, people of all skin colours marched under their slogans and moral leadership. At the height of the protests in June 2020, a poll found 60 per cent of Americans trusted BLM 'to promote justice and equal treatment for people of all races', compared to 56 per cent who trusted US law enforcement to do the same.[4] Global media debated their views on racism. Corporations scrambled to align with them and be seen to be doing so. Governments (re)committed to racial equality; a commission to investigate racial disparities was set up by the UK government. Statues of Confederate generals were brought down in America and of slave traders in Britain. To say anything critical of Black Lives Matter during that summer was widely seen as basically siding with the racists, such was the moral authority they attained. All this helped further a moral atmosphere around race that had been building since Trump's shock 2016 victory, which was widely and rightly seen as a reaction to the Obama presidency.

Today, if I were to mention in my university that I considered a racially ambiguous comment made by a white colleague to be racist, that colleague would likely find themselves on the moral back foot. The default position of most others would be that the comment *must* have been racist if I perceived it as such. Because, in the current moral atmosphere around race, I am, by virtue of my skin colour, invested with a certain authority to decide what constitutes racism and what doesn't.

Even if that colleague did not believe they'd said anything racist and even if many black people might agree that what they said wasn't racist, he or she would likely apologise to me just to be on the safe side. My university, meanwhile, would get worried if I decided to escalate things by taking to Twitter to portray the incident as evidence of a wider racist trend at York. If that got picked up by media outlets, it could be the beginning of a serious PR headache for them.

To be sure, this kind of atmosphere does not exist in every UK working environment and many racial minorities complain about *unambiguously* racist comments at work, as plenty of surveys show.[5] But such an atmosphere does exist in academia and many other professional spaces. It is an atmosphere that offers racial minorities an upper hand over our white colleagues, who will bend over backwards not to have the word 'racist' associated with them in any context whatsoever. Some because they genuinely believe it to be the biggest evil in our world today, others because they simply know how career-damaging such accusations can be.

As with any kind of power, there will always be those who abuse this moral advantage, even if just for emotional satisfaction. White Westerners continue to underappreciate how badly bruised the egos of others have been by the humiliating histories of colonialism and slavery combined with the knowledge whites are still positioned above them today. Most minorities in the West may not think about this on a daily basis, but there's an *awareness* of it at the back of their minds. That awareness can easily morph into a strong emotion once a situation occurs that brings race to the fore. The Floyd killing was an extreme example of such a situation, as were the reactions to it. In everyday life, such situations could include obvious discrimination, a racial comment or even just a look perceived as conveying a sense of superiority.

The human ego always nudges us to exact revenge on those who have offended or hurt us if we get the opportunity. A white colleague saying something that *could* be construed as racist provides an opportunity for us to deliver a moral as well as intellectual reprimand. We can tell them to go 'educate' themselves on racism, history, Africa, or whatever issue their comment concerned. We can wag our fingers at them and say they need to 'do better'. After centuries of them talking down to us, this can be sweetly satisfying as it is only from a moral and intellectual high ground that adults can tell other adults to educate themselves and do better. We can finally be as condescending to them as they have been to us, and if they complain about this, we can always say they are resorting to racist tropes about us being uppity.

Our acknowledged authority on anything to do with race provides us the opportunity to impose a moral hierarchy that positions us at the top and them at the bottom, an inversion of the material hierarchy. We can lay claim to pole position in this moral order, never explicitly of course, always implicitly, by emphasising our historical sufferings at their immoral hands. The temptation to lord it over our white colleagues in this sphere can be a strong one indeed. It is a power to be able to make others squirm, and that is exactly what people do when they are put on the moral defensive.

It is not too surprising that with moral power often being the only kind available to racial minorities in the West, most support those who help sustain the current atmosphere around race, even if they dislike their methods. In the middle of the 2020 BLM protests, just over half – 51 per cent – of Britain's racial minorities felt attacks on statues and memorials in the UK were examples of 'political correctness gone mad', compared with 22 per cent who felt they were in order. Nevertheless, the vast majority – 73 per cent – generally supported the BLM protests.[6] It's like the worker who may not like labour unions and their methods but is happy they're there because they help keep the pressure on management to treat employees fairly. And they are, at the end of the day, employees. Best-case scenario, the unions even negotiate a pay rise that will benefit them personally. It is not in their interests to publicly criticise the unions as that would weaken the latter's position. And what could they possibly gain from *that*?

While this all makes some strategic sense, the problem is that moral power can only go so far in the race equation. For one, this kind of atmosphere around race is restricted to a select few Western nations that are particularly invested in a self-image of justness *and* simultaneously gather detailed race data that can be used as evidence of systemic disparities. Antiracist movements are most visible in the West not because racism doesn't exist elsewhere but because they find it difficult getting attention elsewhere. Moral power can only thrive where the environment is enabling.

As mentioned earlier, Eastern Europeans for the most part simply don't care what black and brown people think about them. A majority of Poles, Czechs, Hungarians, Bulgarians, Romanians, Russians and Ukrainians openly declare they would not be willing to accept a Muslim into their family while majorities in virtually all Western European nations say they would be willing to do so.[7] The Chinese don't really care what others think about them either as long it's not affecting their economic dealings. Brazilian police notoriously deploy lethal violence against poor black Brazilians, yet no antiracist movement there has been able to galvanise enough outrage to end these practices despite *half the country* being of black descent! Again, money plays a part here too as most people outside the West are too preoccupied with economic survival to fight injustices around them.

Meanwhile, the whole idea of a 'Western civilisation' is of a group of societies that see themselves as not just more materially advanced than others but more just as well. This self-image, in combination with a sense of guilt over the past, is why accusations of racism are more likely to get a reaction in the West than anywhere else. And when I say 'the West', we are really speaking of the US and UK plus perhaps to some lesser extent the likes of Canada and Australia.

In Europe, only three nations legally require public bodies to gather systematic data on race and ethnicity – Ireland, Finland and Britain. Despite being home to millions of racial minorities, the likes of Germany and France simply don't gather such data. Without stats backing up their arguments, it is difficult for antiracist organisations there to foster a moral atmosphere around race akin to that in Britain or America. And without moral power, they have virtually no other power to compel the majority into doing anything really, aside from resorting to violence which is unlikely to bring long-term gains for minority groups in any society.

As it stands, racial minorities don't wield much moral power outside the Anglo-American world, and nothing suggests this will change anytime soon. You don't have to be Machiavellian to suspect white establishments in the likes of France and Germany will likely look to racial happenings in Britain and America and double down on *not* gathering race data, knowing the results would likely provide ammunition to those arguing they are racially unequal societies. And if the Anglo-American moral atmosphere cannot be replicated elsewhere, it cannot shift things globally.

Another drawback to relying on moral power is its events-dependent nature. Race was a big issue in the 1960s when Western youths were rebelling against all social conventions in their societies, providing antiracist and anticolonial movements ready support for their causes. But it receded to the background in the 1970s as most colonies had gained independence and Westerners were more worried about economic recessions and that decade's crisis of capitalism. In the 1980s, the Thatcher–Reagan era, Westerners were preoccupied with the Cold War, as cracks in the communist bloc emerged with the rise of pro-democratic movements like Poland's Solidarity.

As for the 1990s, they were a period of intense self-satisfaction for the West following the collapse of the Soviet

Union and communism. It saw its triumph as not just a material victory but a moral one as well. After all, 'Western liberal values' had won the day, as Francis Fukuyama famously declared in *The End of History*. The West was so intoxicated with its success, no one was going to get far suggesting there was something fundamentally wrong with its societies.

Following the 9/11 attacks, a debate erupted in the West around Islam, which by default meant discussing brown (sometimes black) people. But it was focused on religious fundamentalism, not on the role of race in the conflict. It was Barack Obama's historic 2008 campaign that returned race to the forefront of Western debate, this time in a positive tone, with talk of us entering a 'post-racial' world after his thumping election victory. Then we swung back to a 1960s vibe after Trump's 2016 election. The aftermath of the Floyd killing appeared to *cement* a new moral consensus on race, namely that the West remains inherently racist.

But even in this so-called woke era, less than a year after Floyd was killed, attitudes had shifted in the US.[8] The American public's trust in BLM to 'promote justice and equal treatment for people of all races' had fallen from 60 per cent to 50 per cent while their trust in US law enforcement to do the same had *risen* from 56 per cent to 69 per cent. While 60 per cent of Americans described Floyd's death as 'murder' in June 2020, that number had slumped to 36 per cent by March 2021. Meanwhile, white America's support for BLM had fallen back to where it was before Floyd's death – at 37 percent.

While there have been other killings of unarmed black Americans by police since Floyd, none have sparked anything close to the reaction we saw in 2020. The particular reasons for this are less relevant than the fact such moral mood-swings happen often as societies move on to other issues or everyday life. Moral power will thus always be a shaky foundation for any disadvantaged group to build its hopes for better treatment on. Material power is not permanent either, but it is less fleeting than moral power which is wholly dependent on the mood of the public and the powerful. Material power provides a far more solid foundation to negotiate dignity from, not to speak of status.

Paradoxically, even the moral power wielded by British and American antiracists today is heavily reliant on the material power of white progressives. It is the latter who control the global media like CNN, *NYT* and the *Guardian* that are instrumental in amplifying race issues to the mainstream public. They are also the ones who dominate Western academia as discussed earlier. Once other causes start preoccupying the attention of white progressives, and there are always many candidates for their attention, race falls down the media agenda. Twitter alone is not enough to keep your message in the mainstream.

Another shortcoming of a reliance on moral power is that when it is derived from your status as a victim, you need to be perceived as the biggest victim of the day to wield it effectively. This is no easy task in an era of competitive victimhood where at any given time, many disadvantaged groups are jostling to portray their situation as that most deserving of public support. In the summer of 2020, black people were clearly seen as the world's chief victims and support duly flowed in that direction.

But after Russia invaded Ukraine in early 2022, Ukrainians, though white, took over the mantle of the world's chief victims. You can't compete for sympathy with a group being slaughtered by a major military power while putting up a heck of a fight in the process. So just two years after the seemingly epic BLM protests, reports of Ukrainian racism towards African students trying to leave the country after the invasion never triggered much global outrage.[9] The world was focused on the more drastic suffering of Ukrainians. Juxtaposed against their situation, the problems of black people suddenly appeared less terrible in the world's eyes.

Moreover, while victimhood can be a source of moral power, it has the drawback of associating the group with a lack of agency and status, which, again, inspires pity and sympathy but not respect. This is particularly true of long-lasting victimhood. All groups have been conquered or oppressed by some other group at some point in their history, so people get that this can happen to anyone. But if a group has been downtrodden for centuries with no end in sight, people *will* start wondering whether something is 'wrong' with them, including members of the group itself. 'Everywhere you go in Africa the same problems, corruption, bad leaders, poverty. Are we Africans cursed or what?' I've heard such sentiments expressed countless times by exasperated Africans. Self-doubt is common in long-suffering groups.

Some African American antiracists like Ibram X. Kendi, who wields huge moral power on the left, acknowledge that racism is a 'power construct' and must be so tackled. The problem, of course, is how to go about that practically in a scenario where African Americans constitute 13 per cent of the population, which is not small but not huge either. There is no realistic scenario in which black America comes to wield as much material power as white America. Not to speak of the UK where black folk make up just 4 per cent of the population. And the wealth gaps are what they are.

I think the reason many antiracists focus on moral arguments is because they find the starkness of the material power gaps so daunting. How do you catch up in material power with groups who have so much more than yours and are accumulating more as we speak? And what exactly can an American or British antiracist do to stop African countries being the poorest and weakest in the world? Not much, can be one depressing answer.

The moral sphere, on the other hand, is a sphere of words, and words are free. It can seem a far more appealing and hopeful sphere for achievement than the material sphere. The moral atmosphere around race in (some) Western countries is one we can realistically aspire to control by emphasising that we are the only ones with the authority to speak on this subject.

As long as that is accepted by a majority, we can then deploy our resultant moral power to police the language white people use when talking to or about us. You can't say that, this is racist. You can't say this, that is racist. By making sure to keep them on the moral defensive with regular reminders of the past and how racist they continue to be today, we can hold on to power in this sphere. With it, we can negotiate some concessions. Ensure some greater balance at least. Such appears to be the implicit logic.

As for powerful white progressives, there are also some good reasons for them to favour a race debate dominated by moral arguments rather than practical ones. Not only does it cost them nothing, but they can actually make money off it. All they must do is provide column space, book contracts, airtime and endlessly deferential praise to antiracist thinkers of colour. Build up their profiles and sell them to their fellow white progressives. There's a good market for victimhood stories and if you're running the *Guardian* or the *NYT,* you also know there's a lot of rage around race, especially regarding white privilege.

Stories highlighting just how better than the rest of us white people have it inevitably provoke lots of comments, retweets and heated debates. 'Audience engagement' it's called, and media output is often measured by this metric. Race is great for site traffic which is great for ad revenues and so on. Of course, many white progressives are genuinely interested in fighting racism, but that doesn't mean the moral outrage these stories trigger doesn't end up putting more money (and power) in their pockets. And they get to look virtuous in the process. That's about as win-win as it gets.

In the past few decades, there's been a clear shift in the moral dynamics of race relations in Western societies, which have gone from being based on the overt domination of white majorities to one in which most white folk acknowledge a moral responsibility to protect the rights and dignities of minorities. In the context of such a dynamic, moral power *will* continue to be useful in helping ensure this happens in practice and not just on paper.

But it is nowhere near enough to fundamentally change the status quo. For most people of colour in this world, the benefits of the moral atmosphere around race in Britain and America amount to zero. While it offers a few well-positioned minority individuals in the West status and influence in certain spaces, it cannot radically improve the overall position of their collectives. To achieve this will require much more than moral arguments.

11

Future scenarios

I have argued that collective wealth is the foundation which provides groups with the ability to influence events, environments and people in several key domains. It enables some to decide who gets access to the world's best economic opportunities via visa regimes, to lead knowledge and technology production, to spread their ways of thinking, to influence international institutions in ways others can't, to have the standing to allocate global prestige and to have the military capacity to coerce by force if deemed necessary. As of today, whites are the only racial group objectively strong in *all* these spheres via the nations they are majorities in, hence the current order. So, what does the future hold for racial dynamics?

We cannot discuss future scenarios without discussing the demographic shifts the world has undergone and will continue to undergo this century. Demography is destiny, it is often said. Question is: what *kind* of destiny? This century will bring us answers to this in a way few others have.

That the world is undergoing seismic demographic shifts is indisputable. In 1950, 31 per cent of the global population lived in Europe and North America. Today, that proportion has dropped to 17 per cent, and by 2050, it is expected to have shrunk to 13 per cent. In contrast, Africa's share of the world's population has gone in the opposite direction, from under 10 per cent in 1950 to a projected 25 per cent by 2050.[1]

When white people were establishing a racial hierarchy with themselves at the top and black folk at the bottom, they comfortably outnumbered the latter. In less than three decades, there will be three times more black people than white people in the world. Some other non-white groups have also seen their share of the global population grow in the last century and many are hoping these demographic shifts will end the current racial order.

Nowhere are such expectations expressed more often and vocally than in the US, where white Americans' share of the population is expected to drop below 50 per cent in 2045.[2] By then, a quarter of Americans will be Hispanic, 13 per cent will be black, 8 per cent will be of Asian descent and 4 per cent will be multiracial. Considering 90 per cent of America was white in 1945, this is a significant transformation of America's racial profile.

Ever since these projections were first announced a couple of years ago, there have been heated debates on how they will affect America's racial order. These debates provide a good starting point for observations about the wider global picture. Considering America is still the most powerful nation on earth, race dynamics there will certainly have some impact on the rest of us and the issues discussed there reflect those that will continue to be discussed elsewhere.

'Wake up America! Today's minorities will soon be the majority and white people will lose their power,' is the progressive left's general take on these numbers. Consequently, many racial minorities now impatiently look forward to a time when they become the American norm, whites no longer enjoy dominant status and America's racial order is consigned to the dustbins of history. In these Americans, the demographic shifts have provoked an optimism about the future along with a strengthened resentment of the present.

It is one thing to be part of a low-status group in an order that appears insurmountable. The human default in such situations is for resignation to set in and people to get on with their lives as best they can. But it is quite another thing to endure a lower status in an order you have been told is on its deathbed, yet one you are still experiencing. Why can't the order just die *today* is the likelier feeling in such a scenario. Frustration is more painful for those tantalised with its end.

It is in this context that we should interpret the recent focus, even obsession, with whiteness and everything to do with it. 'White people just . . . ', 'White people are like . . . ' Posts starting with these words and then proceeding to some negative evaluation of *white* behaviour often go viral on social media.

While this trend can appear driven by irrational emotions, it reflects a deeper, rational desire to hasten the lowering of white status. Many would like to personally experience a world in which whites are not instinctively positioned above them. Social media, which is all about numbers – the one thing whites no longer have an advantage in – is the ideal platform with which to try and realise this scenario. An African American tweeting about white privilege in America can count on black people elsewhere in the world, including in populous Africa, retweeting their post. The point is to send a message that there are more of us than there are of you on this planet, and we *will* bring you down from that high horse.

On the other side, these demographic shifts, and the expectations they are fostering, are causing significant anxiety among many whites who are angry, depressed or both about the future. Aside from the fact no group likes to hear they are shrinking while others are multiplying, groups that have sat atop an order for a long time come to see their dominant status as somewhat natural. This is not just a white thing but a high-status group thing; the long-time rich in every society feel similarly entitled.

Without all the excited noise around these demographic shifts and what they foretell, it is doubtful there could have been a President Trump. Obama would likely have been viewed as a historical anomaly by white America and the country would have moved on to electing a white establishment president in 2016, as per usual. But a President Obama in combination with all those projections meant many whites sought reassurances they were still in charge and could perhaps remain so in perpetuity. Cue bombastic Trump. However, Joe Biden's decisive 2020 victory with Kamala Harris by his side as his eventual successor has reignited the belief among non-white Americans that white primacy is on its deathbed.

Those with high hopes for a fundamental change in the race equation are resting them on the emergence of a two-bloc society evenly divided between whites and the rest (people of colour). The latter, united in the fact they are not white, will soon have the power to check the white bloc, which will be further split between liberals, who it is hoped are amenable to ending the current order, and conservatives who will be the only group hostile to change. These white conservatives will now be a minority, at most a quarter of the population, unable to block change, and it will finally be possible to build a just America. These calculations are not completely illogical.

It is obviously not in the interests of anyone who is not white for whiteness to retain its higher status vis-à-vis others. This shared interest is a plausible uniting glue for a potential people-of-colour bloc which, in America, the most racially diverse collective on earth, would encompass those who trace their roots to places as different from each other as Nigeria, Nicaragua, Iraq and India.

But even those who would like this scenario to play out have warned things could go a very different way. As far back as 2004, Eduardo Bonilla-Silva, a sociology professor at Duke University and leading antiracist thinker, warned that instead of a white versus rest scenario, the US could move to a Latin American-style tri-racial order sometime this century.[3]

In this scenario, a reconstructed *white* group at the top would include traditional whites, assimilated white Latinos, lighter-skinned multiracials and a few Asian-origin people. A second *honorary white* group would include lighter-skinned Latinos, Indian and Chinese Americans, Middle Eastern Americans, Filipino Americans and most multiracials. Positioned at the bottom would be a *collective black* group that would include blacks and dark-skinned Latinos as well as some other Asian and immigrant groups.

Bonilla-Silva suggested 'objective gaps in income, occupational status, and education between these various groups' could help foster such an order. According to him, '"honorary whites" do better than members of the "collective black", have developed a racial attitudinal profile closer to that of whites and prefer to associate with whites (a preference pattern that is reciprocated) than with members of the "collective black"'. He suggested most Americans would likely accept a tri-racial order as they would find themselves in one of the first two higher-status groups.

In his view, the only way to prevent this from happening was for those who would find themselves in the collective black group to forge a coalition with progressive Asian and Hispanic Americans in 'a concerted effort to politicize "honorary whites" and make them aware of the honorary character of their status'. It needed to be impressed upon them that their intermediate status would always 'be dependent upon whites' wishes and practices'. In other words, it would be reversible and white people would still look down on them no matter what.

This is clearly the strategy being adopted by many of today's antiracist activists who are trying to foster a white versus rest scenario by consistently emphasising that whites look down on everyone who is not white while playing non-white groups off against each other. They designate some as 'model minorities' (*honorary whites*) so they can feel superior to other minorities and accept whatever crumbs whites throw their way. *Don't fall for their divide-and-rule tactics, they are the enemy*, is the general message. Today's racial identity politics, as practised by minorities in the West, boil down to trying to drive home this message.

These alternative US scenarios – a white versus rest equation or a remodelled racial hierarchy – are likely possibilities in the global picture as well. There is also a third possibility; that this century brings us a colour-blind world with no racial hierarchies or competing racial blocs. Race simply ceases to matter, and we start viewing each other as human beings with universal faults and imperfections. This is the scenario wished for by many on the centre-right and centre-left who believe deepening racial polarisation promises nothing but strife and dangerous zero-sum thinking. In my ideal scenario, a colour-blind world would be by far the best option. But the direction things go will depend not on my wishes or that of any other individual, but on the balance between hierarchy-enhancing and hierarchy-attenuating forces at both objective and subjective levels.

What the objective material situation will be in the coming decades no one can say for sure, especially in these uncertain times. But we do have some strong indicators of what it is shaping up to look like, bar unforeseen cataclysmic events. The seven largest emerging economies today, six of which are in the global South, are projected to overtake the G7 in economic size in the 2030s. This would be a historic turning point in a global economy dominated by Western powers for the last couple of centuries. In 2021, the UK's Department for International Trade acknowledged that 'the world's economic centre of gravity will continue to shift eastward in the decades ahead'.[4]

In the coming decades, more than half of the globe's economic growth is expected to come from the Indo Pacific region, compared with a quarter from the EU and US combined.

As wealth shifts eastwards in combination with significant technological prowess, so will power and status. Of course, 'the East' is a huge combination of nations at various economic levels, but it is looking increasingly likely that the Japanese, Koreans, Singaporeans, Taiwanese and Chinese will soon be joined by the Indians, Indonesians, Turks and others in the ranks of the collectively wealthy or at least relatively so.

Contrary to antiracist narratives trying to entrench a white versus rest scenario, the growing power and status of these groups will not be dependent upon any *permission* from whites who will have little choice but to approach them as equals if they themselves want to keep thriving economically. Just the way 'old-money' European aristocrats could do nothing to stop the nouveau riche in their societies becoming elites in the twentieth century. Wealth means you don't have to ask anybody's permission to become important. The world automatically starts to see you this way, usually because it wants or needs something from you.

Africa's rapid demographic growth has objective implications for the racial future as well. By all indications, the continent will face an uphill struggle to provide enough jobs, food and security for its expanding population in the midst of climate change and a host of other challenges. Under current trends, even though many African economies are expected to experience some solid growth moving forward, Africa is projected to account for just over 4 per cent of global GDP by 2050, even while a quarter of the world's population will live there.

While its demographic expansion will boost wealth, it also means that the wealth created will go towards catering for a significantly larger number of people. As a result, it is projected that by 2050, just one in twenty-five Africans will have attained global middle-class status, compared to one in six South Asians and one in four Latin Americans. While extreme poverty is expected to have been virtually eliminated in Asia and Latin America by mid-century, Africa is headed to be the outlier, with 85 per cent of the poorest billion people on the planet.[5] Even if African countries defy these odds and do twice as well as expected, this will still mean just one in twelve Africans being in the global middle class by 2050 and most of the rest either poor or very poor.

If this negative scenario were to play out, the question would then be how other racial groups would interpret their rising fortunes against those of black Africans and other groups who might not be faring so well. This brings us to the role of the *subjective* in the future race equation; what will be the popular views on how we should understand differences in group outcomes?

Will egalitarian ideals have a greater influence on people's worldviews than the belief the successful are where they are because they are likely in some way better than others and thus deserving of higher status? If we are members of more successful groups, will we stop listening to our collective egos telling us this means we are better? If we are members of less successful groups, will we stop feeling awe for those who are where we'd like to be, elevating their status even further? Will we stop believing we live in a dog-eat-dog world and need to further our own groups' interests to survive? Will our everyday lives give us good cause to stop believing that? Will our deep-rooted commitment to hierarchical thinking have disappeared? Are we likely to have discarded race as an explanatory factor for disparate group outcomes?

I won't pretend to know how people will think in twenty years' time. But here too, we have some helpful indicators to go by. For starters, as these demographic changes unfold in real time, they are likely to continue being reported and discussed vigorously on both right and left, for the reasons earlier mentioned. Whatever keeps race on the agenda works towards entrenching racialised worldviews.

As of today, three-quarters (74 per cent) of black Americans say their racial identity is 'extremely' or 'very' important to how they think about themselves, as do 59 per cent of Hispanic Americans and 56 per cent of Asian Americans.[6] In Britain, 82 per cent of minorities say their racial and ethnic identities are an important part of who they are and two in three believe we don't talk about race enough in Britain.[7] Add to this the growth of an inherently polarising social media culture and the material realities of the world we inhabit, and it becomes clear that the colour-blind scenario is the least likely scenario. Race will most likely continue to matter for the foreseeable future.

What then do the chances of the two other scenarios – white versus rest or remodelled racial hierarchy – resemble? The whites versus rest strategy is a same-boat strategy that rests on whites being perceived as fundamentally different from all other groups and treating all others disparagingly. Current race literature portrayals of 'whiteness' as a unique phenomenon strive to create such a sense of fundamental difference between them and all the rest of us. The hope is that while I may have little in common with my Chinese or Turkish neighbour, if we can both roll our eyes at the behaviour of 'Karens' and white people generally, it would mean a white versus rest worldview is taking hold at some level.

However, for this scenario to triumph, the argument that whites will never see those who are not white as their equals would have to resonate with the lived experiences of many members of other groups. Perhaps this will be the case, but I doubt it.

Overt displays of racism by whites are much rarer today than they were twenty years ago and will likely be even rarer in twenty years' time by when generation Z will be running the world. For people of Indian or Chinese descent to feel they are seen as second-class humans by whites in 2040 would require the 'woke' white generation to have acted out the exact opposite of the ideals it says it believes in today, chief of which is antiracism. What if the generality of whites, who will need to survive in a world in which they are a shrinking minority and where economic power is moving eastwards, are for the most part respectful towards people from those rising groups?

This is a distinct possibility because if history has taught us anything about white Westerners, it is that they are a generally pragmatic bunch who can adapt their behaviour when needs must. Another potential obstacle to a white versus rest order emerging is that there are several non-white groups already displaying more complex understandings of themselves than simply being not-white. I myself have written a book on how mixed-race Britons today perceive themselves and their position in the world. It is quite different from how mixed-race people used to perceive themselves back when there were so few of them that they didn't really have a choice in the matter. And when mixed-race people get married to white people (as three-quarters of them do in Britain), even though their children are technically in the 'people of colour' bloc, they can often look white and identify with whites.

In the US, while many Hispanics are darker-skinned, the majority are lighter-skinned and most consider themselves to be ethnically white. Which is why if you count American whites as those who ticked the 'white only' identity box in the 2020 census, the figure stands at 62 per cent, but if you look at those who identified as 'white' plus another racial identity, the figure jumps to 71 per cent.[8] White identity itself is changing in America. 'I don't see how we can claim that white is a single thing at this point. Perhaps we should say white represents a spectrum more than it does a well-defined group,' suggested Richard Alba, a sociologist at the City University of New York.[9]

Suffice to say, identity is becoming an increasingly complex affair in this century, so sustaining a white versus rest divide may be more difficult than some hope, both for reasons of identity and the unpredictability of future white behaviour towards certain groups.

If I had to bet going by current trends, I would say that due to our generally strongly status-oriented thinking patterns, our deep-rooted reverence for material success, the spread of the ideology of meritocracy which suggests those who do well are more competent, and the influence of our egos, many members of groups rising economically will likely consider themselves better than those from groups doing worse.

I can thus easily imagine a three-tier implicit racial order emerging in the world at large. One with whites and other newly wealthy and successful groups positioned at the top, relatively successful groups somewhere in the middle and the collectively poorest groups persistently positioned at the bottom.

In such a scenario, even far-reaching successes of black folk in the West, who by mid-century will likely constitute less than 5 per cent of the global black population, would be unlikely to overshadow a core image of blackness determined by the condition of its overwhelming majority in Africa. As long as black people remain, on average, significantly much poorer than others, and black nations significantly less developed, blackness will continue to be associated with low status in the eyes of the world. No matter how many times we accuse it of 'racism'.

I realize black folk who grew up in the West will likely consider this unfair and illogical, but the reality is that blackness will always be associated with Africa, its ancestral homeland, just as whiteness will always be associated with Europe. If Europe were to become poor overnight and reliant on aid from countries of the global South, it would not take long for white status to be re-evaluated downwards in the eyes of the world. That is the way human beings operate for now. The question, then, is what would need to happen for a more positive scenario to emerge for blackness this century?

Conclusion:

Africa is the way forward

The extremity of the wealth gap between black and white is what makes it such a potent driver of black–white status differences. To meaningfully disrupt the racial order would thus require significantly narrowing that gap. There are, of course, major wealth disparities between various groups, but I focus on the black–white gap because I see narrowing it as essential to reducing racial frictions in our time. As mentioned, predominantly black Africa will soon constitute a quarter of the world's population. Solve the black–white issue and you solve the race problem. Prejudices of various kinds will always exist, but there wouldn't be an *obvious* racial order causing so much vexation.

If the black–white issue is not faced head on, such frustrations will only grow along with the numbers of the black population. Racial identity politics, fuelled by emotive social media discourse and influencers tapping into mass anger, will gain momentum, irrespective of warnings of its inherent divisiveness. As it gains momentum, so will right-wing (sometimes openly racist) reactions to it, making things ever messier and uglier. 'Emotions are the mechanism that heighten the saliency of a particular concern,' observed Roger Petersen, a political science professor at MIT who studies group conflicts.[1] Provocative social media posts will ensure emotions continue to heighten the status concerns of non-whites as well as of whites worrying what the future holds for *them* in a changing world. Mutual resentment cannot lead to positive outcomes.

As for white folk, if they're worried about their shrinking numbers in proportional terms, they need to start having more children, there's no other solution to this particular concern really. When it comes to alleviating black frustrations, addressing the wealth gap is a practical necessity.

It is not about guilt-tripping anyone, simply about pointing out certain hard facts that are going nowhere. This is not about the past, it is about the future. About the world our children will grow up in, whether it will be a toxic environment of mutually perpetuating resentments or a saner, healthier clime where people can breathe more freely and where more have access to a decent life. I'm not talking Utopia here, just a somewhat less volatile scenario than we currently have. What would need to change for this to happen?

First and foremost, Africa's ruling classes need to start creating the enabling environments Africans require to realise their potential and multiply black wealth. This the *sine qua non* to any meaningful change in the big picture. Not all African states are equally badly or corruptly governed; some are run much better than others. Nevertheless, what is undeniable is that Africans expect and need much stronger states, with better-functioning institutions and a lot less corruption. Without better quality governance, capitalism will never enrich us collectively as it has enriched others. There's no dancing around this basic truth.

However, leaving the issue at 'you guys need to sort yourselves out and get rich' is unlikely to suffice. While despair is not an option, neither is fantasy. Suggesting Africa could catch up with the rich world if it only started being better governed is fantasy.

Unlike China, it is obviously not a single country ruled by a stable authoritarian regime that can implement five-year plans, suppress workers' wages, and generally stifle their populations to keep capital happy and forthcoming. It is fifty-four countries at varying levels of development with states that often have limited control over their populations. States often way more culturally diverse, and thus difficult to manage, than is appreciated. States with citizenries highly sceptical of their governments thanks to past disappointments. There's really no point asking whether Africa will be 'the next China' as many Western headlines have done in recent years. It won't.

Some African nations will do better than others going forward, but for now there is no massive incentive for global firms to, say, shift their manufacturing from Vietnam or China (where many are still ready to work for much less than in the West) to Nigeria or Kenya. The Western and East Asian pathway to mass job creation through manufacturing is thus unlikely for Africa, at least not on the scale needed to absorb its rapidly expanding workforce.

Taken as a whole, Africa today simply does not have the financial muscle to tackle its many problems on its own, not to speak of the issues connected to climate change and other phenomena beyond its control. Aside from better governance, it requires three fundamentals for dynamic wealth creation:

education, infrastructure and capital.

It requires a Marshall Plan in all three spheres. In thirty-four African countries surveyed in 2021, an average 17 per cent of adults had attended institutions of higher learning, 37 per cent had completed secondary school, 27 per cent had only a primary-school education while 20 per cent of adults reported having no formal education whatsoever.[2] This will clearly not do in a world where over fifty per cent of young adults aged 25-34 have a tertiary education in the likes of Britain or South Korea. With 60 per cent of Africans currently under the age of twenty-five, it is the youngest continent in the world; giving that young population the proper skills to navigate the twenty-first century is key here.

A Marshall Plan for education would involve training thousands of new teachers and building thousands of new schools. It would involve ensuring good-quality, near-free education at primary- and secondary-school levels as well as accessible tertiary education. Countries like Rwanda, Nigeria and others are already cooperating with the likes of Microsoft to build 'smart' classrooms, complete with computers, internet connectivity and basic software packages. Such efforts need to be intensified and expanded. This will require money.

Many young African adults are already taking charge of their futures, coming up with innovative solutions to problems in their environment, as discussed in the chapter on technology and race. African youths display stunning levels of entrepreneurial spirit. More than three in four of those aged eighteen to twenty-four have plans to start their own business within the next five years.[3] What they often lack is access to capital, which 61 per cent of African youths cite as the single greatest barrier to them establishing a business.

When a 2022 survey asked Africa's youths what they would do if given $100, half said they would invest in or start a business, 17 per cent said they would save it, 12 per cent said they would invest it in their education.[4] Just 5 per cent said they would spend it on fun, a remarkably low figure for a survey carried out among eighteen to twenty-four-year-olds. Africa's young know what they need to do to improve their lives. Encouragingly, two-thirds believe their country is creating a culture of innovation and entrepreneurship and increasing access to the digital economy. Filling that capital void while training them how to manage businesses would go a long way in boosting the continent's economic prospects.

Better infrastructure in terms of roads, railways and things like internet accessibility is another basic needed. There has been significant progress on this front in many parts of Africa in recent years, largely thanks to infrastructure partnerships with the Chinese. But more is required, especially for such fast-growing populations.

The whole world is currently experiencing a cost-of-living crisis. Those at the bottom half of Western societies often own little and are 'Jams' (just about managing) themselves. This is clear. However, rich-country governments, multinational corporations and the other half of rich-country citizens do still wield significant resources between them, as has been highlighted in this book.

A combination of support from these three sets of actors could help fuel the needed process of wealth creation on the African continent. In the sphere of what individuals can do, there are eight billion people in the world; if just one per cent of them chose to contribute towards the cause for racial economic equality – FREE – that would be eighty million donors. Even if people contributed modest sums, that would give the potential to raise billions.

White progressives are often members of the upper-middle classes in the West and can play a significant role here. Simply waxing deferential towards people of colour in books, articles and debates is not going to end the racial order. Without the power of money to change the fundamentals of global race dynamics, slogans about racial justice and equality will remain just that. To argue, for instance, that the burden of narrowing the racial wealth hierarchy rests solely with Western governments and one-per-centers would be to try and avoid personal cost by shifting the responsibility onto someone else. It would be to always look for a 'them' that need to sort things out, to argue for a just world so long as someone else pays for it.

Multinationals of course have much deeper pockets than individuals, as do rich governments. I realise trust is an issue here. 'Billions of aid money has gone into Africa in recent decades, so much of which has been lost to corruption. Why would this be anything different?' some may well ask. That is a perfectly legitimate question. However, I think things are going to be different going forward because of an impending game-changer in Africa's power dynamics: biology. Many African nations are still being run by a generation of septuagenarians who have been calling the shots for the past few decades. Most will soon join their creator, to be replaced by a younger generation of leaders.

Africa's younger elites get the kind of arguments I have been making in this book in a way that older generation did not. That generation believed *personal* wealth could guarantee them global status even if the countries they ruled were left poor and underdeveloped. They believed that amassing fortunes and buying mansions in Europe's most expensive neighbourhoods would ensure they were looked at with the same eye white elites were looked at. They were mistaken. Yes, their (often stolen) wealth was happily banked by smiling Westerners and mansions were readily sold to them, but that never meant they were respected. For what but contempt could be the attitude of anyone to those who would rob their own blind to fund a lifestyle of ostentatious luxury?

Africa's incoming elites are a better-travelled generation, people who have been around the world, mixed with others and know exactly how they see Africa, and why. They realise personal wealth cannot shield them from the global nation-based hierarchy. As Peter Obi, a recent Nigerian presidential candidate who captured the imagination of many young Nigerians, observed, 'If you're from a poor country, you're poor, no matter how rich you are. When abroad, once you say where you're from, people class you based on that.' Hence, according to Obi, himself a multimillionaire, 'everyone from Nigeria is poor'.

People now get that the only pathway to global respect for Africans and black people in general is a collectively strong and successful Africa. While it would be silly of me to suggest the continent will soon be run by angels (who don't run any government here on earth last I checked), it will be run by people who realise things must change in order for Africa to be competitive in the global arena. If just for them to be able walk with their heads high in that global arena. It is thanks to this palpable realisation of what must be done for Africans to be respected that we can reasonably expect to see less of the kind of wasteful corruption than we have in the past.

And to stay pragmatic, it would likely be wise for as much as possible of whatever funds raised for such an initiative to be forwarded *directly* to African citizens to limit the potential for government corruption. In these days of mobile money transfers and most people having bank accounts, this is technically doable.

Better trade deals would also be helpful. While one cannot expect any country to negotiate deals that would not benefit its own citizens, when considering the consequences of such agreements with African countries, the rich world should not be too short-term in its thinking. Yes, today you have the economic muscle to dictate the terms of trade agreements pretty much, but the multiplication of poverty in Africa is not in your long-term interests as it will only make for a more volatile world. Which is bad for everyone and everything, including business.

All said and done, our collective future rests on the ability of today's rich and powerful to structure the global economy in a manner conducive to its poorest members becoming richer. Africa should not be seen as a problem to be solved, but as the solution to a problem. The race problem. A richer Africa will make for an easier world to live in for all, for both material and psychological reasons. The knowledge there are successful black nations would go a long way in making black people in the West less defensive in their everyday interactions with white folk. Less touchy about their status in the world.

As it stands, white wealth, and black lack of it, creates a whole set of dynamics that are highly unhealthy for race relations, as I have tried to show in this book. Altering those dynamics will require some serious work on one side and sacrifice on the other. It will not be easy, but it is the only plausible pathway to smoother race relations and a better future for all that I see for now.

Acknowledgements

I would like to thank all the folk at Little, Brown who believed in this book and helped me work on it, especially Andreas and Holly who have been indispensable. Matthew, thanks for being a great agent. I would also like to thank every single writer and thinker who has discussed the race issue before me and whose work I have been fortunate to come across. I have benefited from all your ideas, including those I have disagreed with as they have forced me to come up with good reasons for disagreeing! How *good* those reasons have been, I leave to the judgement of the reader. Either way, THANK YOU.

Notes and references

Introduction: What children see

1 Shutts, Kristin, Katherine D. Kinzler, Rachel C. Katz, Colin Tredoux, and Elizabeth S. Spelke. 2011. 'Race Preferences in Children: Insights from South Africa.' *Developmental Science* 14 (6): 1283–91. https://doi.org/10.1111/j.1467-7687.2011.01072.x.

2 Olson, Kristina R., Kristin Shutts, Katherine D. Kinzler, and Kara G. Weisman. 2012. 'Children Associate Racial Groups with Wealth: Evidence from South Africa.' *Child Development* 83 (6): 1884–99. https://doi.org/10.1111/j.1467-8624.2012.01819.x.

3 Ibid.

4 Shutts, Kristin, Elizabeth L. Brey, Leah A. Dornbusch, Nina Slywotzky, and Kristina R. Olson. 2016. 'Children Use Wealth Cues to Evaluate Others.' Edited by Marina A. Pavlova. *PLoS ONE* 11 (3): e0149360. https://doi.org/10.1371/journal.pone.0149360.

5 Ahl, Richard E., and Yarrow Dunham. 2017. '"Wealth Makes Many Friends": Children Expect More Giving from Resource-Rich than Resource-Poor Individuals.' *Child Development* 90 (2): 524–43. https://doi.org/10.1111/cdev.12922.

6 Ibid.

7 Greene, Richard Allen. 2020. 'Black and White Britain Miles Apart on Racism, CNN Poll Finds.' www.cnn.com, June 22, 2020. https://edition.cnn.com/interactive/2020/06/europe/britain-racism-cnn-poll-gbr-intl/.

8   Singh, Matt. 2020. 'Stephen Lawrence: Has Britain Changed?' Number Cruncher Politics. July 20, 2020. https://www.ncpolitics.uk/2020/07/stephen-lawrence-has-britain-changed/.

9   Ipsos MORI. 2021. 'Public Perceptions of Institutional Racism Key Findings.' https://www.ipsos.com/sites/default/files/ct/news/documents/2021-07/Public%20perceptions%20of%20institutional%20racism%20report_Ipsos%20MORI_FINAL_July%202021.pdf.

10 Pew Research Center. 2021. 'Deep Divisions in Americans' Views of Nation's Racial History - and How to Address It.' Pew Research Center. August 12, 2021. https://www.pewresearch.org/politics/wp-content/uploads/sites/4/2021/08/PP_2021.08.12_racial-attitudes_REPORT.pdf.

11 Pew Research Center. 2019. 'About Half of Blacks Say Being Black Has Hurt Their Ability to Get Ahead.' *Pew Research Center's Social & Demographic Trends Project*. May 2, 2019. https://www.pewresearch.org/social-trends/psdt_03-25-19_race_update-17/.

12 *BBC News*. 2022. 'BBC Africa Eye Expose: Chinese Man Held over Racist Videos.' June 20, 2022. https://www.bbc.co.uk/news/world-africa-61862619.

13 Prabhu, Maya. 2017. 'African Victims of Racism in India Share Their Stories.' www.aljazeera.com, May 3, 2017. https://www.aljazeera.com/features/2017/5/3/african-victims-of-racism-in-india-share-their-stories.

14 United Nations. 2021. 'New Report Calls for Transformative Action for Racial Justice.' OHCHR. June 28, 2021. https://www.ohchr.org/en/stories/2021/06/new-report-calls-transformative-action-racial-justice.

15 Paice, Edward. 2022. 'By 2050, a Quarter of the World's People Will Be African - This Will Shape Our Future.' *The Guardian*, January 20, 2022. https://www.theguardian.com/global-development/2022/jan/20/by-2050-a-quarter-of-the-worlds-people-will-be-african-this-will-shape-our-future.

1. A picture of racial wealth

1   European Network Against Racism. 2019. 'ENAR's Election Analysis - Ethnic Minorities in the New European Parliament 2019-2025.' European Network against Racism. June 4, 2019. https://www.enar-eu.org/enar-s-election-analysis-ethnic-minorities-in-the-new-european-parliament-2019/.

2   Jones, Nicholas, Rachel Marks, Roberto Ramirez, and Merarys Rios-Vargas. 2021. 'Improved Race and Ethnicity Measures Reveal U.S. Population Is Much More Multiracial.' The United States Census Bureau. August 12, 2021. https://www.census.gov/library/stories/2021/08/improved-race-ethnicity-measures-reveal-united-states-population-much-more-multiracial.html.

3   International Monetary Fund. 2021. Imf.org. https://www.imf.org/External/Datamapper/NGDPD@WEO/WEOWORLD.' www.imf.org.

4   Koop, Avery. 2021. 'Mapped: GDP per Capita Worldwide.' Visual Capitalist. July 26, 2021. https://www.visualcapitalist.com/mapped-gdp-per-capita-worldwide/.

5   Ibid.

6   Department For International Trade. 2021. 'Global Trade Outlook.' https://assets.publishing.service.gov.uk/government/uploads/system/uploads/attachment_data/file/1036243/global-trade-outlook-september-2021.pdf.

7   Credit Suisse. 2019. 'Global Wealth Report.' https://www.credit-suisse.com/about-us/en/reports-research/global-wealth-report.html.

8   Onuah, Felix, and Chijioke Ohuocha. 2021. 'Nigeria Cranks up Spending to Record $39.8 Bln in 2022 Budget.' Reuters, October 7, 2021. https://www.reuters.com/world/africa/nigeria-unveils-record-398-bln-budget-2022-spending-up-25-2021-10-07/.

9   Beniwal, Vrishti, and Archana Chaudhary. 2021. 'India's $500 billion Budget to Spur Growth Leaves Little for the Poor.' www.Bloomberg.com, February 2, 2021. https://www.bloomberg.com/news/articles/2021-02-01/-500-billion-india-budget-to-spur-growth-leaves-little-for-poor?leadSource=uverify%20wall.

10 Reuters. 2022. 'Slovak Budget Gap Narrows to 7 Bln Euros in 2021,' January 3, 2022. https://www.reuters.com/markets/rates-bonds/slovak-budget-gap-narrows-7-bln-euros-2021-2022-01-03/.

11 Kidd, Carla. 2020. 'Household Wealth by Ethnicity, Great Britain - Office for National Statistics.' www.ons.gov.uk. November 23, 2020. https://www.ons.gov.uk/peoplepopulationandcommunity/personalandhouseholdfinances/incomeandwealth/articles/householdwealthbyethnicitygreatbritain/april2016tomarch2018.

12 Bhutta, Neil, Andrew C. Chang, Lisa J. Dettling, and Joanne W. Hsu with assistance from Julia Hewitt. 2020. 'Disparities in Wealth by Race and Ethnicity in the 2019 Survey of Consumer Finances.' www.federalreserve.gov. September, 2020. https://www.federalreserve.gov/econres/notes/feds-notes/disparities-in-wealth-by-race-and-ethnicity-in-the-2019-survey-of-consumer-finances-20200928.html.

13 Long, Heather. 2020. 'The Black-White Economic Divide Is as Wide as It Was in 1968.' *The Washington Post*, June 4, 2020. https://www.washingtonpost.com/business/2020/06/04/economic-divide-black-households/.

14 German, Freire, Carolina Diaz-Bonilla, Steven Schwartz Orellana, Jorge Soler Lopez, and Flavia Carbonari. 2018. 'Afro-Descendants in Latin America,' August, 2018. https://openknowledge.worldbank.org/handle/10986/30201.

15 GOV.UK. 2019. 'Income Distribution.' Service.gov.uk. July 26, 2019. https://www.ethnicity-facts-figures.service.gov.uk/work-pay-and-benefits/pay-and-income/income-distribution/latest.

16 U.S. Bureau Of Labor Statistics. 2018. 'Asian Women and Men Earned More than Their White, Black, and Hispanic Counterparts in 2017.' Bls.gov. August 29, 2018. https://www.bls.gov/opub/ted/2018/asian-women-and-men-earned-more-than-their-white-black-and-hispanic-counterparts-in-2017.htm.

17 Matthews, Dylan. 2018. 'The Massive New Study on Race and Economic Mobility in America, Explained.' *Vox*, March 21, 2018. https://www.vox.com/policy-and-politics/2018/3/21/17139300/economic-mobility-study-race-black-white-women-men-incarceration-income-chetty-hendren-jones-porter.

18 *Time*. 1962. 'South Africa: Honorary Whites.' January 19, 1962. https://content.time.com/time/subscriber/article/0,33009,895835,00.html.

2. Attitudes to money

1 World Inequality Database. 2020. 'Global Inequality Data - 2020 Update.' WID - World Inequality Database. November 10, 2020. https://wid.world/news-article/2020-regional-updates/.

2 Zitelmann, Rainer. 2022. 'Attitudes towards the Rich in China, Japan, South Korea, and Vietnam.' *Economic Affairs* 42 (2): 210–24. https://doi.org/10.1111/ecaf.12524.

3   Ibid.

4   Nel, Philip. 2021. 'Why Africans Tolerate Income Inequality.' *The Journal of Modern African Studies* 59 (3): 343–65. https://doi. org/10.1017/s0022278x21000161.

5   Omolaoye, Sodiq. 2022. 'Diaspora Remittances Hit $20b, Says NIDCOM.' *The Guardian Nigeria*, July 22, 2022. https://guardian.ng/ business-services/diaspora-remittances-hit-20b-says-nidcom/.

6   Wike, Richard, Jacob Poushter, Janell Fetterolf, and Shannon Schumacher. 2020. 'Little Trust Worldwide in Trump's Handling of International Affairs.' Pew Research Center's Global Attitudes Project. January 8, 2020. https://www.pewresearch.org/global/2020/01/08/little-trust-in-trumps-handling-of-international-affairs/.

3. Visa power

1   UN Migration. 2020. *World Migration Report 2022.* International Organization for Migration. https://publications.iom.int/books/world-migration-report-2022.

2   GOV.UK. 2020. 'An Inspection of the Home Office's Network Consolidation Programme and the 'Onshoring' of Visa Processing and Decision Making to the UK.' GOV.UK. February 6, 2020. https://www. gov.uk/government/publications/an-inspection-of-the-home-offices-network-consolidation-programme-and-the-onshoring-of-visa-processing-and-decision-making-to-the-uk.

3   Passport Index. 2022. 'Global Passport Power Rank | the Passport Index 2022.' Passport Index - All the World's Passports in One Place. 2022. https://www.passportindex.org/byRank.php.

4   Department for International Trade. 2021. 'Global Trade Outlook.' https://assets.publishing.service.gov.uk/government/uploads/system/ uploads/attachment_data/file/1036243/global-trade-outlook-september-2021.pdf.

5   'The Intolerant Left.' *The Atlantic*, November 14, 2017. https://www. theatlantic.com/entertainment/archive/2017/11/the-intolerant-left/545783/.

6   Esipova, Neli, Anita Pugliese, and Julie Ray. 2018. 'More than 750 Million Worldwide Would Migrate If They Could.' Gallup.com.

December 10, 2018. https://news.gallup.com/poll/245255/750-million-worldwide-migrate.aspx.

7 Pew Research Center. 2018. 'At Least a Million Sub-Saharan Africans Moved to Europe since 2010.' Pew Research Center's Global Attitudes Project. March 22, 2018. https://www.pewresearch.org/global/2018/03/22/at-least-a-million-sub-saharan-africans-moved-to-europe-since-2010/.

8 Nwaubani, Adaobi. 2022. 'The Nigerians Hoping to Check out of Their Country.' *BBC News*, March 1, 2022. https://www.bbc.co.uk/news/world-africa-60393076.

9 The European Business Council for Africa. 2022. 'EBCAM - African Youth Survey 2022.' www.ebcam.eu. June 27, 2022. https://www.ebcam.eu/publications/reference-reports-and-documents/3029-african-youth-survey-2022.

10 World Economic Forum. 2022. 'Why Africa's Youth Hold the Key to Its Development Potential.' World Economic Forum. September 19, 2022. https://www.weforum.org/agenda/2022/09/why-africa-youth-key-development-potential/#:~:text=Today%2C%20more%20than%2060%25%20of.

11 Kariba, Felix. 2020. 'The Burgeoning Africa Youth Population: Potential or Challenge? | Cities Alliance.' Cities Alliance. 2020. https://www.citiesalliance.org/newsroom/news/cities-alliance-news/%C2%A0burgeoning-africa-youth-population-potential-or-challenge%C2%A0.

12 UNCTAD. 2021. 'Facts and Figures | UNCTAD.' unctad.org. 2021. https://unctad.org/press-material/facts-and-figures-7.

13 United Nations. 2019. 'UNIVERSAL HUMAN RIGHTS INDEX.' ohchr.org. 2019. https://uhri.ohchr.org/en/.

14 The Law Society. 2021. 'Budget Response: Justice System given Crucial Investment.' www.lawsociety.org.uk. October 27, 2021. https://www.lawsociety.org.uk/Contact-or-visit-us/Press-office/Press-releases/Budget-response-Justice-system-given-crucial-investment.

15 Ernst & Young. n.d. 'Tanzania Budget Highlights.' Accessed November 9, 2022. https://assets.ey.com/content/dam/ey-sites/ey-com/en_tz/ey-tz-budget-assests/ey-tanzania-budget-speech-2022-23-newsletter.pdf.

16 European Union Agency for Fundamental Rights. 2023. 'Being Black in the EU: Experiences of People of African Descent' https://fra.europa.

eu/sites/default/files/fra_uploads/fra-2023-being-black_in_the_eu_
en.pdf.

17 UN News. 2019. 'More than 90 per Cent of Africa Migrants Would
    Make Perilous Europe Journey Again, despite the Risks.' UN News.
    October 21, 2019. https://news.un.org/en/story/2019/10/1049641.

18 Ipsos. 2021a. 'Broken-System Sentiment in 2021.' https://www.ipsos.com/
    sites/default/files/ct/news/documents/2021-07/GA%20-%20Broken%20
    System%20Sentiment%20-%20Populist%20Anti-Elitism%20and%20
    Nativism%20in%202021%20-%20Graphic%20Report.pdf.

4. Respect

1 Finley, Taryn. 2016. 'Black Lives Matter Founder Alicia Garza
   Responds to Dallas Shooting.' *HuffPost UK*. July 9, 2016. https://www.
   huffingtonpost.co.uk/entry/black-lives-matter-alicia-garza-dallas-
   shooting_n_578105c4e4b0344d514f834c.

2 Cuddy, Amy J.C., Susan T. Fiske, and Peter Glick. 2008. 'Warmth
   and Competence as Universal Dimensions of Social Perception: The
   Stereotype Content Model and the BIAS Map.' Edited by Mark Zanna.
   In *Advances in Experimental Social Psychology*, 61–149. https://doi.
   org/10.1016/s0065-2601(07)00002-0.

3 Ibid.

4 Brand Finance. 2022. 'Global Soft Power Index.' https://brandi-
   rectory-live-public.s3.eu-west-2.amazonaws.com/reports_free/
   brand-finance-soft-power-index-2022.pdf.

5 Ibid.

6 Bergh, Robin, Gregory K. Davis, Sa-kiera T. J. Hudson, and Jim
   Sidanius. 2019. 'Social Dominance Theory and Power Comparison.'
   Social Comparison, Judgment, and Behavior. 575–97. https://doi.
   org/10.1093/oso/9780190629113.003.0020.

7 Ibid.

8 Horwitz, Donald L. 1985. *Ethnic Groups in Conflict*. Berkeley,
   California; London: University of California Press.

9 GOV.UK. 2022. 'EU Settlement Scheme Quarterly Statistics, June
   2022.' GOV.UK. September 27, 2022. https://www.gov.uk/govern-
   ment/statistics/eu-settlement-scheme-quarterly-statistics-june-2022/

eu-settlement-scheme-quarterly-statistics-june-2022#:~:text=In%20
total%2C%20there%20were%206%2C120%2C800.

10 Office For National Statistics. n.d. 'Population of the UK by Country of
Birth and Nationality - Office for National Statistics.' www.ons.gov.uk.
Accessed November 9, 2022. https://www.ons.gov.uk/peoplepopula-
tionandcommunity/populationandmigration/internationalmigration/
bulletins/ukpopulationbycountryofbirthandnationality/yearending-
june2021#:~:text=Polish%20has%20been%20the%20most.

11 Fiske, Susan T. 2018. 'Stereotype Content: Warmth and Competence
Endure.' *Current Directions in Psychological Science* 27 (2): 67–73.
https://doi.org/10.1177/0963721417738825.

12 Glaeser, Edward L., Rafael Di Tella, and Lucas Llach. 2018. 'Introduction
to Argentine Exceptionalism.' *Latin American Economic Review* 27 (1).
https://doi.org/10.1007/s40503-017-0055-4.

5. How Western academia sustains white status

1 Adekoya, Remi, Eric Kaufmann, and Thomas Simpson. 2020.
'Academic Freedom in the UK Protecting Viewpoint Diversity.' https://
policyexchange.org.uk/wp-content/uploads/2022/10/Academic-
freedom-in-the-UK.pdf.

2 QS Top Universities. 2022. 'QS World University Rankings 2022.'
Top Universities. 2022. https://www.topuniversities.com/university-
rankings/world-university-rankings/2022.

3 Shanghai Ranking. 2022. 'Shanghai Ranking's Academic Ranking of
World Universities.' www.shanghairanking.com. 2022. https://www.
shanghairanking.com/rankings/arwu/2022.

4 Kerr, Emma. 2014. '10 Universities with the Biggest Endowments.' US
News & World Report. 2014. https://www.usnews.com/education/
best-colleges/the-short-list-college/articles/10-universities-with-the-
biggest-endowments.

5 University of York. 2021. 'Summary of Funding and Expenditure.' York.
ac.uk. 2021. https://www.york.ac.uk/about/funding-and-expenditure/.

6 'Education Fund: Leaving No Child Behind – 2021 Education Budget
Analysis – BudgIT.' n.d. Www.readkong.com. Accessed November 9,
2022. https://www.readkong.com/page/education-fund-leaving-no-child-
behind-2021-education-8750750.

7   Ibid.

8   Davies, Leslie, and Richard Fry. 2019. 'College Faculty Have Become More Racially and Ethnically Diverse but Remain Far Less so than Students.' Pew Research Center. July 31, 2019. https://www.pewresearch. org/fact-tank/2019/07/31/us-college-faculty-student-diversity/.

9   Brothers, Patrick. 2019. 'Ten Charts That Explain the Global Education Technology Market.' *Medium*. February 24, 2019. https://medium. com/@patrickbrothers/ten-charts-that-explain-the-global-education-technology-market-6809fa68484c.

10 Project Atlas. 2020. 'Explore Data.' Www.iie.org. 2020. https://www.iie. org/en/Research-and-Insights/Project-Atlas/Explore-Global-Data.

11 Stacey, Viggo. 2022. 'UK Hits 600,000 Target 10 Years Early – HESA.' thepienews.com. January 25, 2022. https://thepienews.com/news/ uk-hits-600000-10-years-early/.

12 Parliament.uk. 2013. 'House of Lords – Persuasion and Power in the Modern World – Select Committee on Soft Power and the UK's Influence.' Publications.parliament.uk. 2013. https://publications.parliament.uk/pa/ ld201314/ldselect/ldsoftpower/150/15008.htm.

13 Openshaw, Hannah. 2009. 'New Evidence Shows Commonwealth Scholarships Benefit UK Society.' Commonwealth Scholarship Commission in the UK. November 5, 2009. https://cscuk.fcdo.gov. uk/new-evidence-shows-commonwealth-scholarships-benefit-uk-society/.

14 Higgins, James. 2021. 'UK Universities Educated 57 Serving World Leaders, Soft-Power Index Reveals.' University Business. September 2, 2021. https:// universitybusiness.co.uk/international/uk-universities-educated-57-serving-world-leaders-soft-power-index-reveals/.

15 Ibid.

6. Technology and race

1   Falola, Toyin. 2010. *The Power of African Cultures*. Rochester: University of Rochester Press.

2   HM Government. 2021. 'Global Britain in a Competitive Age: the Integrated Review of Security, Defence, Development and Foreign Policy.' https://assets.publishing.service.gov.uk/government/uploads/system/

uploads/attachment_data/file/975077/Global_Britain_in_a_Competitive_ Age-_the_Integrated_Review_of_Security__Defence__Development_ and_Foreign_Policy.pdf.

3   Maddison, Angus. 2001. 'The World Economy: A Millennial Perspective.' Development Centre Studies. https://theunbrokenwindow.com/ Development/MADDISON%20The%20World%20Economy--A%20 Millennial.pdf.

4   Ibid.

5   World Intellectual Property Organization. 2022. 'Global Innovation Index 2022, 15th Edition.' www.wipo.int. September 29, 2022. https:// www.wipo.int/global_innovation_index/en/2022/.

6   Ponciano, Jonathan. 2022. 'The World's Largest Tech Companies in 2022: Apple Still Dominates as Brutal Market Selloff Wipes Trillions in Market Value.' Forbes, May 12, 2022. https://www.forbes.com/ sites/jonathanponciano/2022/05/12/the-worlds-largest-technology-companies-in-2022-apple-still-dominates-as-brutal-market-selloff-wipes-trillions-in-market-value/?sh=7ca4a9a43448.

7   Onukwue, Alexander. 2021. 'What Tech Hubs Have Achieved in Africa in the Last Decade.' Quartz, December 14, 2021. https://qz.com/ africa/2102189/what-tech-hubs-have-achieved-in-africa-in-the-last-decade.

8   Kigotho, Wachira. 2021. 'Countries Spend Less than 1% of GDP on Research.' University World News. June 17, 2021. https://www. universityworldnews.com/post.php?story=20210616151534847.

9   Chen, Stephen. 2022. 'China Resumes R&D Push with Record US$441 Billion Outlay in 2021.' South China Morning Post, February 9, 2022. https://www.scmp.com/news/china/science/article/3166424/china-resumes-rd-push-record-us441b-outlay-2021.

10 Yonhap. 2022. 'S. Korea Ranks 2nd among OECD Nations in R&D Spending as Portion of GDP: Report.' The Korea Herald, April 20, 2022. https://www.koreaherald.com/view.php?ud=20220420000141.

11 'African Scientists Sign Open Letter Calling for Increased R&D Funding.' 2021. The Africa Report.com, December 15, 2021. https:// www.theafricareport.com/156852/african-scientists-sign-open-letter-calling-for-increased-rd-funding/.

12 Mikati, Azmi. 2022. '2.9 Billion People Have No Internet, Mainly Marginalized Women.' POLITICO, September 7, 2022. https://www.

politico.eu/sponsored-content/2-9-billion-people-have-no-internet-mainly-marginalized-women/.

13 'UAE Internet Statistics 2021.' 2022. Official GMI Blog. August 30, 2022. https://www.globalmediainsight.com/blog/uae-internet-statistics/.

14 Benson, Emmanuel Abara. 2022. '15 Countries with the Lowest Internet Penetration in Africa.' *Business Insider Africa*, July 6, 2022. https://africa.businessinsider.com/local/markets/15-countries-with-the-lowest-internet-penetration-in-africa/gpm8kc7.

15 Benjamin, Ruha. 2019. *Race after Technology: Abolitionist Tools for the New Jim Code*. Medford, Ma: Polity.

16 Hogenboom, Melissa. 2018. 'What Does Your Accent Say about You?' *bbc.com*. *BBC Future*. 2018. https://www.bbc.com/future/article/20180307-what-does-your-accent-say-about-you.

17 Accent Bias Britain. 'Results: Labels.' n.d. Accent Bias Britain. https://accentbiasbritain.org/results-labels/.

18 Harwell, Drew. 2019. 'Federal Study Confirms Racial Bias of Many Facial-Recognition Systems, Casts Doubt on Their Expanding Use.' *The Washington Post*, December 19, 2019. https://www.washingtonpost.com/technology/2019/12/19/federal-study-confirms-racial-bias-many-facial-recognition-systems-casts-doubt-their-expanding-use/.

19 Ibid.

20 Anand, Priya, and Ellen Huet. 2021. 'Why Silicon Valley's Many Asians Still Feel Like A Minority.' *www.bloomberg.com*, August 6, 2021. https://www.bloomberg.com/news/features/2021-08-06/why-silicon-valley-s-asian-americans-still-feel-like-a-minority.

21 Ibid.

22 PricewaterhouseCoopers. n.d. 'PwC's Global Artificial Intelligence Study: Sizing the Prize.' PwC. https://www.pwc.com/gx/en/issues/data-and-analytics/publications/artificial-intelligence-study.html#:~:text=AI%20could%20contribute%20up%20to.

23 PricewaterhouseCoopers. n.d. 'The Impact of 5G: Creating New Value across Industries and Society.' PwC. https://www.pwc.com/gx/en/about/contribution-to-debate/world-economic-forum/the-impact-of-5g.html#:~:text=The%20key%20functional%20drivers%20of.

7. Western media, the news arm of whiteness?

1   Gathara, Patrick. 2021. 'In Journalism, Language Matters.' www.aljazeera.com, October 3, 2021. https://www.aljazeera.com/opinions/2021/10/3/language-matters-in-journalism.

2   Makura, Moky. 2022. 'Opinion: Media Coverage of Ukraine Shows It's Time to Rethink What We Know about Africa.' CNN, March 4, 2022. https://edition.cnn.com/2022/03/03/opinions/racist-media-coverage-ukraine-africa-makura-lgs-intl/index.html.

3   Bayoumi, Moustafa. 2022. 'They Are 'Civilised', 'European' and 'Look like Us': The Racist Coverage of Ukraine.' *The Guardian*, March 2, 2022. https://www.theguardian.com/commentisfree/2022/mar/02/civilised-european-look-like-us-racist-coverage-ukraine.

4   Hannan, Daniel. 2022. 'Vladimir Putin's Monstrous Invasion Is an Attack on Civilisation Itself.' *The Telegraph*, February 26, 2022. https://www.telegraph.co.uk/news/2022/02/26/vladimir-putins-monstrous-invasion-attack-civilisation/.

5   Bhaya, Abhishek. 2022. 'African, Middle Eastern Journalists' Bodies Call out Western Media's 'Racist' Ukraine Coverage.' News.cgtn.com, March 2, 2022. https://news.cgtn.com/news/2022-03-02/African-Arab-journalists-call-out-media-s-racist-Ukraine-coverage-184TmWrJVte/index.html.

6   BBC Media Centre. 2021. 'BBC on Track to Reach Half a Billion People Globally ahead of Its Centenary in 2022.' www.bbc.co.uk, November 24, 2021. https://www.bbc.co.uk/mediacentre/2021/bbc-reaches-record-global-audience.

7   Sharma, Mihir. 2022. 'The U.K. Shouldn't Disarm Itself in the Soft-Power War.' www.Bloomberg.com, January 21, 2022. https://www.bloomberg.com/opinion/articles/2022-01-21/the-bbc-is-the-u-k-s-biggest-soft-power-weapon.

8   Majid, Aisha. 2022. 'Most Popular Websites for News in the World: Monthly Top 50 Listing.' *Press Gazette*, March 2, 2022. https://pressgazette.co.uk/most-popular-websites-news-world-monthly/.

9   Ramachandran, Naman. 2022. 'BBC Posts Record Income of $6.4 Billion, Welcomes "Informed Debate" on Future Funding Model.' *Variety*, July 12, 2022. https://variety.com/2022/tv/global/bbc-income-2021-2022-1235314430/.

10 SABC. n.d. 'SABC Annual Report 2021/22.' Accessed November 9, 2022. http://web.sabc.co.za/digital/stage/corporateaffairs/SABC_Annual_Report_2021_-_2022.pdf.

8. International influence

1   'House of Lords – Persuasion and Power in the Modern World – Select Committee on Soft Power and the UK's Influence.' n.d. Publications. parliament.uk. https://publications.parliament.uk/pa/ld201314/ldselect/ldsoftpower/150/15008.htm.

2   Novosad, Paul, and Eric Werker. 2018. 'Who Runs the International System? Nationality and Leadership in the United Nations Secretariat.' *The Review of International Organizations* 14 (1): 1–33. https://doi.org/10.1007/s11558-017-9294-z.

3   Jahic, Naida. 2022. 'How Norway's Foreign Aid Programs Are Fighting Global Poverty.' The Borgen Project. September 28, 2022. https://borgenproject.org/norways-foreign-aid-programs/.

4   Kanamugire, Johnson. 2022. 'Rwanda Budget Goes Big in Bid to Clear Debt, Pay Covid Bills.' *The East African*, February 8, 2022. https://www.theeastafrican.co.ke/tea/business/rwanda-to-increase-2021-2022-budget-3709158.

5   Babatunde, Aishat. 2020. 'Nigeria Underfunding Diplomatic Missions, Weakening Foreign Policy-Experts.' *Premium Times Nigeria*, December 11, 2020. https://www.premiumtimesng.com/news/headlines/430537-nigeria-underfunding-diplomatic-missions-weakening-foreign-policy-experts.html.

6   'Is China Contributing to the United Nations' Mission? | ChinaPower Project.' 2018. ChinaPower Project. August 3, 2018. https://chinapower.csis.org/china-un-mission/.

7   Hyde, Andrew. 2022. 'China's Emerging Financial Influence at the UN Poses a Challenge to the U.S.' Stimson Center. April 4, 2022. https://www.stimson.org/2022/chinas-emerging-financial-influence-at-the-un/.

8   International Monetary Fund. n.d. 'IMF – International Monetary Annual Report 2016.' www.imf.org. https://www.imf.org/external/pubs/ft/ar/2016/eng/quota.htm.

9   Weisbrot, Mark, and Jake Johnston. 2016. 'Voting Share Reform at the IMF: Will It Make a Difference?' Center For Economic And Policy Research. https://cepr.net/images/stories/reports/IMF-voting-shares-2016-04.pdf.

10 International Monetary Fund. n.d. 'IMF Executive Directors and Voting Power.' IMF. https://www.imf.org/en/About/executive-board/eds-voting-power.

11 Kim, Soo, and Jesslene Lee. 2020. 'Gaining Ground, Gaining Influence? Vote Shares and Power in the AIIB.' Political Economy of International Organization. https://www.peio.me/wp-content/uploads/2020/02/PEIO13_paper_100_1.pdf.

12 'China Is Biggest Stumbling Block in India's UNSC Permanent Membership.' 2020. *Hindustan Times*, November 19, 2020. https://www.hindustantimes.com/india-news/china-is-biggest-stumbling-block-in-india-s-unsc-permanent-membership/story-yTpTstOwjEY7vYz5t2NiNN.html.

13 Brown, William, and Sophie Harman, eds. 2013. *African Agency in International Politics*. London; New York: Routledge, Taylor & Francis Group.

14 Goldenberg, Suzanne. 2006. 'Bush Threatened to Bomb Pakistan, Says Musharraf.' *The Guardian*, September 22, 2006. https://www.theguardian.com/world/2006/sep/22/pakistan.usa.

15 Peçanha, Sergio, and Keith Collins. 2018. 'Only 5 Nations Can Hit Any Place on Earth with a Missile. For Now.' *The New York Times*, February 7, 2018. https://www.nytimes.com/interactive/2018/02/07/world/asia/north-korea-missile-proliferation-range-intercontinental-iran-pakistan-india.html?mtrref=www.google.com&assetType=PAYWALL&mtrref=www.nytimes.com&gwh=BBDD3CAE62EF466CCB6242D1A191C2C2&gwt=pay&assetType=PAYWALL.

16 Béraud-Sudreau, Lucie, Alexandra Marksteiner, Xiao Liang, Diego Lopes da Silva, and Nan Tian. 2022. 'Trends in World Military Expenditure, 2021.' SIPRI. April 1, 2022. https://www.sipri.org/publications/2022/sipri-fact-sheets/trends-world-military-expenditure-2021.

17 International Campaign to Abolish Nuclear Weapons. n.d. 'South Africa.' ICAN. https://www.icanw.org/south_africa.

18 Ahmed, Kaamil. 2020. 'Ending World Hunger by 2030 Would Cost $330bn, Study Finds.' *The Guardian*, October 13, 2020. https://www.theguardian.com/global-development/2020/oct/13/ending-world-hunger-by-2030-would-cost-330bn-study-finds.

9. The feminisation of white power

1   Cain, Sian. 2015. 'Man Booker Winner Marlon James: "'Writers of Colour Pander to the White Woman.'" *The Guardian*, November 30, 2015. https://www.theguardian.com/books/2015/nov/30/marlon-james-writers-of-colour-pander-white-woman-man-booker-event-brief-history-seven-killings.

2   Flood, Alison. 2016. 'Publishing Industry Is Overwhelmingly White and Female, US Study Finds.' *The Guardian*, January 27, 2016. https://www.theguardian.com/books/2016/jan/27/us-study-finds-publishing-is-overwhelmingly-white-and-female.

3   ——. 2020. 'US Publishing Remains "'as White Today as It Was Four Years Ago.'" *The Guardian*, January 30, 2020. https://www.theguardian.com/books/2020/jan/30/us-publishing-american-dirt-survey-diversity-cultural-appropriation.

4   Publishers Association. 2021. 'Diversity Survey of the Publishing Workforce 2020.' Publishers Association. February 11, 2021. https://www.publishers.org.uk/publications/diversity-survey-of-the-publishing-workforce-2020/.

5   Books + Publishing. 2022. 'How International Book Markets Performed in 2021.' February 23, 2022. https://www.booksandpublishing.com.au/articles/2022/02/23/210379/how-international-book-markets-performed-in-2021/#:~:text=According%20to%20research%20from%20the.

6   The Authors Guild. 2022. 'Book Sales Up, Readership Down.' January 25, 2022. https://authorsguild.org/news/book-sales-up-readership-down/.

7   Barron, Kaelyn. 2022. 'Top 15 Publishers by Revenue: Who Earned the Most in 2021?' TCK Publishing. May 8, 2022. https://www.tckpublishing.com/top-publishers-by-revenue/.

8   So, Richard Jean, and Gus Wezerek. 2020. 'Just How White Is the Book Industry?' *The New York Times*, December 11, 2020. https://www.nytimes.com/interactive/2020/12/11/opinion/culture/diversity-publishing-industry.html.

9   FTSE Women Leaders. 2022. 'FTSE Women Leaders Review Achieving Gender Balance.' https://ftsewomenleaders.com/wp-content/uploads/2022/05/2021_FTSE-Women-Leaders-Review_Final-Reportv1_WA.pdf.

10 Syed, Nurhuda. 2020. 'Why Is HR a Female-Dominated Profession?' www.hcamag.com. April 29, 2020. https://www.hcamag.com/us/specialization/diversity-inclusion/why-is-hr-a-female-dominated-profession/221057.

11 Fischer, Ronald, Katja Hanke, and Chris G. Sibley. 2012. 'Cultural and Institutional Determinants of Social Dominance Orientation: A Cross-Cultural Meta-Analysis of 27 Societies.' *Political Psychology* 33 (4): 437–67. https://doi.org/10.1111/j.1467-9221.2012.00884.x.

12 Pratto, Felicia, Jim Sidanius, and Shana Levin. 2006. 'Social Dominance Theory and the Dynamics of Intergroup Relations: Taking Stock and Looking Forward.' *European Review of Social Psychology* 17 (1): 271–320. https://doi.org/10.1080/10463280601055772.

13 Sidanius, Jim, Sarah Cotterill, Jennifer Sheehy-Skeffington, Nour Kteily, and Héctor Carvacho. 2016. 'Social Dominance Theory: Explorations in the Psychology of Oppression.' In *The Cambridge Handbook of the Psychology of Prejudice*, edited by Chris G. Sibley and Fiona Kate Barlow, 149–87. Cambridge Handbooks in Psychology. Cambridge: Cambridge University Press. doi:10.1017/9781316161579.008.

14 Ibid.

15 Mendelewitsch, Melanie. 2015. 'Eric Zemmour: The Rush Limbaugh of France.' *Observer*, February 10, 2015. https://observer.com/2015/02/eric-zemmour-the-rush-limbaugh-of-france/.

16 Lorimer, Rona. 2022. 'Softbois in France: A Feminist Perspective on the Rise of Éric Zemmour.' *The Conversationalist*, February 3, 2022. https://conversationalist.org/2022/02/03/softbois-in-france-the-rise-of-eric-zemmour-from-a-feminist-perspective/.

17 World Values Survey Association. 2020. 'WVS Database.' www.worldvaluessurvey.org. 2020. https://www.worldvaluessurvey.org/wvs.jsp.

18 Earle, Samuel. 2018. '"Rivers of Blood:"' the Legacy of a Speech That Divided Britain.' *The Atlantic*, April 20, 2018. https://www.theatlantic.com/international/archive/2018/04/enoch-powell-rivers-of-blood/558344/.

10. Moral power

1   Burns, James Macgregor. 1978. *Leadership*. New York: Harper & Row.

2   Ndlovu-Gatsheni, Sabelo J. 2013. 'The Entrapment of Africa within the Global Colonial Matrices of Power.' *Journal of Developing Societies* 29 (4): 331–53. https://doi.org/10.1177/0169796x13503195.

3   United Nations. 1948. 'Universal Declaration of Human Rights.' United Nations. 1948. https://www.un.org/en/about-us/universal-declaration-of-human-rights.

4   Ipsos. 2021. 'Americans' Trust in Law Enforcement, Desire to Protect Law and Order on the Rise.' https://www.ipsos.com/sites/default/files/ct/news/documents/2021-03/usat-ipsos_racial_injustice_topline_030421.pdf.

5   Kudsia Batool. 2022. 'Racism Is Rife in UK Workplaces.' www.tuc.org.uk. August 31, 2022. https://www.tuc.org.uk/blogs/racism-rife-uk-workplaces.

6   Hope Not Hate. 2020. 'A Study of BAME Opinion: Minority Communities in the Time of COVID and Protest.' https://hopenothate.org.uk/wp-content/uploads/2020/08/BAME-report-2020-08-v3-00000003.pdf.

7   Pew Research Center. 2018. 'Eastern and Western Europeans Differ on Importance of Religion, Views of Minorities, and Key Social Issues.' Pew Research Center's Religion & Public Life Project. October 29, 2018. https://www.pewresearch.org/religion/2018/10/29/eastern-and-western-europeans-differ-on-importance-of-religion-views-of-minorities-and-key-social-issues/.

8   Ibid.

9   Dovi, Vivienne. 2022. '"If You Are Black You Can Walk"': Africans Are Facing Racism in Ukraine.' *Euronews*, April 1, 2022. https://www.euronews.com/2022/04/01/the-treatment-africans-are-facing-in-ukraine-is-despicable-but-why-are-we-surprised.

11. Future scenarios

1   Paice, Edward. 2022. 'By 2050, a Quarter of the World's People Will Be African – This Will Shape Our Future | Edward Paice.' *The Guardian*, January 20, 2022. https://www.theguardian.com/global-development/2022/jan/20/by-2050-a-quarter-of-the-worlds-people-will-be-african-this-will-shape-our-future.

2   Frey, William H. 2018. 'The US Will Become 'Minority White' in 2045, Census Projects.' Brookings. March 14, 2018. https://www.brookings. edu/blog/the-avenue/2018/03/14/the-us-will-become-minority-white-in-2045-census-projects/.

3   Bonilla-Silva, Eduardo. 2004. 'From Bi-Racial to Tri-Racial: Towards a New System of Racial Stratification in the USA.' *Ethnic and Racial Studies* 27 (6): 931–50. https://doi.org/10.1080/0141987042000268530.

4   Department for International Trade. 2021. 'Global Trade Outlook.' https://assets.publishing.service.gov.uk/government/uploads/system/ uploads/attachment_data/file/1036243/global-trade-outlook-september-2021.pdf.

5   HM Government. 2021. 'Global Britain in a Competitive Age: the Integrated Review of Security, Defence, Development and Foreign Policy.' https://assets.publishing.service.gov.uk/government/uploads/system/ uploads/attachment_data/file/975077/Global_Britain_in_a_Competitive_Age-_the_Integrated_Review_of_Security__Defence__Development_and_Foreign_Policy.pdf.

6   Barroso, Amanda. 2020. 'Most Black Adults Say Race Is Central to Their Identity and Feel Connected to a Broader Black Community.' Pew Research Center. February 5, 2020. https://www.pewresearch.org/ fact-tank/2020/02/05/most-black-adults-say-race-is-central-to-their-identity-and-feel-connected-to-a-broader-black-community/.

7   Hope Not Hate. 2020. 'A Study of BAME Opinion: Minority Communities in the Time of COVID and Protest.' https://hopenothate.org.uk/ wp-content/uploads/2020/08/BAME-report-2020-08-v3-00000003. pdf.

8   US Census Bureau. 2021. '2020 Census Illuminates Racial and Ethnic Composition of the Country.' Census.gov. August 12, 2021. https:// www.census.gov/library/stories/2021/08/improved-race-ethnicity-measures-reveal-united-states-population-much-more-multiracial. html#:~:text=The%202020%20Census%20shows%20(Figures.

9   Wang, Hansi. 2021. 'This Is How the White Population Is Actually Changing Based on New Census Data.' NPR.org. August 22, 2021. https://www.npr.org/2021/08/22/1029609786/2020-census-data-results-white-population-shrinking-decline-non-hispanic-race.

NOTES AND REFERENCES

Conclusion: Africa is the way forward

1   Petersen, Roger D. 2006. *Understanding Ethnic Violence: Fear, Hatred, and Resentment in Twentieth-Century Eastern Europe.* Cambridge: Cambridge University Press.

2   Amakoh, Kelechi. 2022. 'Declining Performance: Africans Demand More Government Attention to Educational Needs.' Africa Portal. March 15, 2022. https://www.africaportal.org/publications/declining-performance-africans-demand-more-government-attention-educational-needs/.

3   The European Business Council for Africa. 2022. 'EBCAM - African Youth Survey 2022.' www.ebcam.eu. June 27, 2022. https://www.ebcam.eu/publications/reference-reports-and-documents/3029-african-youth-survey-2022.

4   Ibid.

Index

INDEX

INDEX